Makerspaces

⊚ About the Series

This innovative series written and edited for librarians by librarians provides authoritative, practical information and guidance on a wide spectrum of library processes and operations.

Books in the series are focused, describing practical and innovative solutions to a problem facing today's librarian and delivering step-by-step guidance for planning, creating, implementing, managing, and evaluating a wide range of services and programs.

The books are aimed at beginning and intermediate librarians needing basic instruction/guidance in a specific subject and at experienced librarians who need to gain knowledge in a new area or guidance in implementing a new program/service.

⊚ About the Series Editor

The **Practical Guides for Librarians** series was conceived by and is edited by M. Sandra Wood, MLS, MBA, AHIP, FMLA, Librarian Emerita, Penn State University Libraries.

M. Sandra Wood was a librarian at the George T. Harrell Library, The Milton S. Hershey Medical Center, College of Medicine, Pennsylvania State University, Hershey, PA, for over 35 years, specializing in reference, educational, and database services. Ms. Wood worked for several years as a Development Editor for Neal-Schuman Publishers.

Ms. Wood received a MLS from Indiana University and a MBA from the University of Maryland. She is a Fellow of the Medical Library Association and served as a member of MLA's Board of Directors from 1991 to 1995. Ms. Wood is founding and current editor of *Medical Reference Services Quarterly*, now in its 35th volume. She also was founding editor of the *Journal of Consumer Health on the Internet* and the *Journal of Electronic Resources in Medical Libraries* and served as editor/co-editor of both journals through 2011.

Titles in the Series

1. *How to Teach: A Practical Guide for Librarians* by Beverley E. Crane
2. *Implementing an Inclusive Staffing Model for Today's Reference Services* by Julia K. Nims, Paula Storm, and Robert Stevens
3. *Managing Digital Audiovisual Resources: A Practical Guide for Librarians* by Matthew C. Mariner
4. *Outsourcing Technology: A Practical Guide for Librarians* by Robin Hastings
5. *Making the Library Accessible for All: A Practical Guide for Librarians* by Jane Vincent
6. *Discovering and Using Historical Geographical Resources on the Web: A Practical Guide for Librarians* by Eva H. Dodsworth and L. W. Laliberté
7. *Digitization and Digital Archiving: A Practical Guide for Librarians* by Elizabeth R. Leggett
8. *Makerspaces: A Practical Guide for Librarians* by John J. Burke

Makerspaces
A Practical Guide for Librarians

John J. Burke

PRACTICAL GUIDES FOR LIBRARIANS, No. 8

ROWMAN & LITTLEFIELD
Lanham • Boulder • New York • Toronto • Plymouth, UK

Published by Rowman & Littlefield
4501 Forbes Boulevard, Suite 200, Lanham, Maryland 20706
www.rowman.com

10 Thornbury Road, Plymouth PL6 7PP, United Kingdom

British Library Cataloguing in Publication Information Available

Library of Congress Cataloging-in-Publication Data
Burke, John (John J.)
  Makerspaces : a practical guide for librarians / John J. Burke.
      pages cm. — (Practical guides for librarians ; no. 9)
  Includes bibliographical references and index.
  ISBN 978-1-4422-2967-9 (cloth : alk. paper) — ISBN 978-1-4422-2968-6 (ebook)
1. Libraries—Activity programs. 2. Libraries and community. 3. Makerspaces. 4. Do-it-yourself work. 5. Workshops. I. Title.
  Z716.33.B87 2014
  027—dc23
                                                                            2014011171

♾™ The paper used in this publication meets the minimum requirements of American National Standard for Information Sciences—Permanence of Paper for Printed Library Materials, ANSI/NISO Z39.48-1992. Printed in the United States of America

To my wife, Lynne,
and my children,
Madeline, Anna, Philip, and Andrew.

Contents

List of Figures and Tables

⊚ Figures

⊚ Tables

List of Library Makerspace Profiles

Preface

Welcome to *Makerspaces: A Practical Guide for Librarians*! This work is all about librarians choosing to serve their communities by incorporating creative activities in their libraries, perhaps culminating in a formal makerspace. Makerspaces are combinations of a community of users, a collection of tools, and a desire to create, exchange knowledge, and share what is created. The defining character of a makerspace is that it enables making. In this book, you will find questions to ask, examples to explore, tools to use, and best practices to implement on the way to supporting making in your library.

The book began as an exploration into library makerspaces in which I hoped to learn what these spaces are and why they are so compelling. Along the way, I thought that many other librarians are probably undertaking the same journey of discovery or wishing that they had the time to do so. I was compelled to gather and provide in this volume what I have learned and what so many people have taken the time to share.

Makerspaces in libraries involve people: the people who are intrigued by the idea of making, the people who come to programs and open lab times, and the people who support creative efforts. Understanding making's appeal to people in our libraries' communities and helping them to build communities for sharing their explorations and learning from each other is a wonderful mission for libraries.

Makerspaces in libraries involve tools and technologies. This book offers an introduction to many types of making. From ancient practices to the most high-tech accomplishments, the library makerspace can offer a wide range of activities to engage makers. You will leave this book with an increased understanding of what making can be and how it is accomplished.

Makerspaces in libraries involve structure—the structure that undergirds the free-flowing creative spirit that each maker brings into the space. Librarians will learn how to research, seek input, plan, and keep developing a makerspace. The support role that libraries and their staff members can provide to makers is wide open and needs to be defined to ensure that the makerspace is effective and sustainable.

Finally, makerspaces in libraries are about making. The desire to create can awake in a library makerspace and drive makers to pursue all manner of projects. In doing so, they will learn the practical skills of bringing a product into being and be inspired to learn more. Making can create a virtuous cycle of learning and making that benefits the individual, one's making community, and the world. I hope that you will leave the book curious about exploring multiple ways of making and enthused to make something.

One exciting facet of the book is that it profiles 17 library makerspaces throughout the chapters. These librarians are engaged in the work of sharing making technologies and activities with their communities. Each offers advice to those who are starting or continuing to build their own makerspaces.

Makerspaces: A Practical Guide for Librarians contains 12 chapters:

Chapter 1, "The Library as a Creation and Collaboration Space," offers a definition of makerspaces and examines their key characteristics. It suggests why the historical mission of libraries coincides so well with the intent of making.

Chapter 2, "The Maker Movement and Building Up a Making Mind-Set," provides an overview of the history of making things and describes the changes in that process in the current day. The maker movement and its history are defined, with the goal of considering why libraries should become part of the movement.

Chapter 3, "An Overview of Makerspace Implementations," details the process of starting a makerspace, with an emphasis on engaging the library's community. It covers questions to consider when planning and implementing your makerspace.

Chapter 4, "What Will Patrons Make in Your Makerspace?" explores which technologies and making activities libraries are featuring in their makerspaces. It then discusses how to gather ideas and input on the palette of making that your library should pursue.

Chapter 5, "Budgeting for a Makerspace," addresses the financial side of makerspaces. It shares methods for creating a budget and finding funding for the operation of the makerspace.

Chapter 6, "Resources for Audio, Image, and Video Creation," turns from the structure of the makerspace into the actual making that can happen there. It compares options for making audio, image, and video products.

Chapter 7, "Resources for Crafts and Artistic Pursuits," identifies creative activities that can be pursued in the makerspace. It displays a blend of handmade and machine-made opportunities to pursue.

Chapter 8, "Resources for Electronics, Robotics, and Programming," notes the many options available for entry-level and advanced makers to learn facets of electronics, robots, and programming. There are many interesting interplays among these three areas, as well as activities that reach beyond the circuit board.

Chapter 9, "Resources for 3D Printing and Prototyping," takes on the poster child of makerspaces: the 3D printer. The chapter includes 3D-printing options in devices, designs, and materials.

Chapter 10, "Resources for the Unexpected: Lesser-Known Making," addresses making options that do not yet share the spotlight. The twin themes of this chapter are that sometimes less is more with making and that anything is possible in makerspaces.

Chapter 11, "Approaches for Developing a Makerspace That Enables Makers," recommends options for offering makerspace workshops and programs and suggests ways to get wider participation from your community. It also looks at the possible stages of development for a makerspace once it has started.

Chapter 12, "Remaking the Library? Tracking the Present and Future of Making in Libraries," recommends resources for you to consult if you would like to investigate making further. It also conjectures about the growth and development of makerspaces in the years to come.

Finally, *Makerspaces* includes an appendix with the results from a 2013 survey of makerspaces in libraries, a comprehensive bibliography of sources for more information, and a helpful index to topics discussed throughout the book.

Makerspaces are a growing service in libraries, and I hope that this book serves as a helpful resource for you as you start your makerspace or as you look for ways to build your activities. Please let me know if you have question or comments by e-mailing me at techcompanion@gmail.com.

Acknowledgments

I would like to thank the library staff at the Gardner-Harvey Library for their support and encouragement during the process of writing this book. Working with these individuals has taught me much about serving our patrons and not rushing too far ahead with my crazy ideas.

My understanding of the breadth and depth of library makerspaces was greatly increased by the 17 individuals who shared their stories in the profiles. I appreciate their taking time to talk with me and to pass their wisdom on to everyone who reads the book.

My thanks also go to my editor Sandy Wood, who kept me on track and attended to all the essentials needed to bring this work to completion.

Above all, I thank God, the first maker, who strengthens me daily and accepts me just as I am.

CHAPTER 1

The Library as a Creation and Collaboration Space: An Introduction

IDEALAB. MAKEIT TIME. MAKERSPACE. CreateSpace. Innovative Media Space. The Nest. What are these places? They are known collectively as *makerspaces*, *hackerspaces*, or *fab labs* (Cavalcanti 2013). These are places where practical and artistic creations can be made to gain economic, educational, and social rewards. They may be focused on a particular type of technology or activity or equipped with tools for several modes of creative work. They have existed in various forms over the years, sponsored by tech companies, educational institutions, small business incubators, and the collective action of creative hobbyists and programmers. Now they are beginning to find a place in libraries as a laboratory where students can augment science education with practical experiments, as a community workshop where the mingling of multiple creative minds and their respective talents can inspire innovation, or as a collection of often expensive equipment that can be used by all.

Libraries serve a variety of purposes: maintainer of local information sources, community meeting space, study zone, and connector of people and information of all kinds.

Fab labs: focused on prototyping physical products and designs using a combination of digital and physical tools.

Hackerspaces: initially focused on computer programmers and hackers as a place to share computers, socialize, and collaborate.

Makerspaces: spaces used by people to share tools, knowledge, and ideas.

Source. Wikipedia, "Hackerspace," October 27, 2013, http://en.wikipedia.org/wiki/Hackerspace; Chris Anderson, *Makers* (New York: Crown Business, 2012).

Many of the library's core functions have centered on giving people access to materials that they could not find or afford on their own. As many books and other resources have become available in digital form, libraries have changed their spaces to accommodate uses beyond physical item storage: from collaborative study spaces to meeting areas to more space for computers. This trend of reshaping library spaces may have one more turn to take—one that tilts the work of libraries from information consumers and providers to information creators.

What if a library had an area in it where patrons could make something? More than just a computer lab, where students write research papers and adults build résumés or where anyone can create a presentation with cloud-based software—instead, a space that is dedicated to both the tools for making and the discovery of talents for creativity and design, where people can make digital or physical items using tools and equipment that they do not own and where they can receive guidance on using them. This takes libraries on a path related to their traditional role of sharing expensive resources to increase knowledge but this time toward releasing the potential of patrons to create. By providing the space and the means of making, libraries can spur learning, invention, creativity, and innovation.

ⓢ Defining the Makerspace

Finding a definition for the concept of makerspaces is much akin to the blind men who attempted to identify an elephant. For them, the impression gained from feeling a part of the creature was taken to be indicative of its entirety. The man who touched the tail judged that the elephant was very much like a rope, while the man who encountered the trunk believed the elephant to be like a snake. Every man was correct in part but missed the larger picture and the larger truth, not to mention the size of the elephant.

So, too, can the makerspace be defined in ways that are driven by limited experience and that do not give the observer a full sense of what is possible. If a person imagines that makerspaces are all about 3D printers, then this is true in part. There are several makerspace applications for 3D printing: from prototyping models of products to re-creating historical artifacts to building replacement parts for a lawnmower out of plastic. If someone expects makerspaces to involve computer programming or robotics, then that view is also accurate to a degree. Programming and robotics work are happening in makerspaces for kids with LEGOs and for adults with a variety of devices. If an individual shares that makerspaces might have something to do with weaving or sculpture or welding, then those might also be valid conclusions. Unbelievable artwork and materials created by talented hands come from makerspaces that have potter's wheels, soldering, and looms. This train of *if*s could continue ad nauseam, delineating all manner of technologies and creative arts. However, it is only fair to follow each *if* statement with a *but*: "but that is only one vision of what makerspaces can be."

This book explores in great detail the expanding definition of makerspaces and their possibilities. At the conclusion, a clearer and fuller image of these entities should be in mind. Rather than concentrate on wholeness from the outset of this journey, perhaps it is best to understand the nature of makerspaces at their most elemental. The site Makerspace.com (2013) offers this explanation of its namesake: "A collection of tools does not define a makerspace. Rather, it is defined by what it enables: making." Making is the essential outcome of these spaces; a product must ensue from the work in the space.

⑥ Understanding the Development of Makerspaces

So how did we get here? What made makerspaces happen? We might first imagine the individual inventor or tinkerer working in one's laboratory, shop, or garage. In that environment, the act of creation is in the hands of an individual or perhaps a small team. This arrangement allows for easy access to tools for that individual or group but keeps them from easily sharing tools and ideas with others. As well, the tools themselves provide the means for that inventor or group to bring an idea or discovery into being. We can picture the lone inventor coming out of nowhere with a product that fundamentally changes everything that we know.

Getting those tools out into a common space where multiple inventors could come together and share their knowledge is an important breakthrough that makerspaces provide. The knowledge sharing becomes crucial and time-saving to those who hope to learn to make; yet, it also has a profound impact on those who know more but can still benefit from new perspectives and from the learning process that comes from teaching others.

This aspect owes its start to an earlier and continuing form of makerspace called the *hackerspace*. Early hackerspaces were places formed by computer hackers—a culture of computer users dedicated to learning about computer systems by taking programs apart and rebuilding them (Levy 2010). These hackers would use the space to talk about their individual projects, suggest solutions to one another, and then perhaps collaborate on larger programming efforts. This model allows for independence in direction for each person involved but provides a community to turn to for ideas and guidance.

In addition to the community-sharing element of the makerspace, access to tools cannot be understated. While individual inventors come from a range of economic classes, they build their collections of machinery and tools to meet their own needs—from their own incomes. Gathering tools for common use or borrowing allows individuals to learn how to use them and make things with them without incurring excessive expenses along the way. Anyone might be able to compile a set of handy tools (e.g., hammers, screwdrivers, saws) over time at no more than a few tens of dollars per item. But purchasing

Figure 1.1. Noisebridge makerspace in San Francisco. *Image provided through a CC BY 2.0 License by Kyle Nishioka (madmarv00), http://www.flickr.com/photos/madmarv/8798768470/*

a drill press, a laser cutter, or a 3D printer takes hundreds or thousands of dollars. Makerspaces allow for a big investment in equipment to be shared by many individuals, and those individuals have the freedom to experiment with equipment that they may or may not need until they find the right device to enable their making. You can see how the combination of tools might look in figure 1.1.

Describing Makerspaces

With two key aspects of makerspaces established—knowledge sharing and tool sharing—here are four other key characteristics of makerspaces, all of which are explored in the coming chapters.

Hands-On Learning and Exploration

Makerspaces may have classes to teach people how to use a particular tool or technology, but in general they are not home to a planned curriculum for learning. The goal of makerspaces is to provide the items and guidance needed to a maker so that one can explore and create at will. A maker starts with an idea, then follows through the process of creation oneself, with one's own hands.

Coworking

Coworking means what it says: working with others on projects. Perhaps you and others are working together on the same project or on separate projects but in the same place.

> **TEXTBOX 1.2.**
>
> ## WHAT MAKERSPACES ARE MADE OF
>
> Shared knowledge
>
> Shared tools
>
> Hands-on learning and exploration
>
> Coworking
>
> STEM education focus
>
> Maker culture—share your stuff!

It is drawn from the hackerspace model noted earlier. Working in a makerspace means working in an environment where you are not just formally taught by others but inspired by their creations—and where you add your own inspiring reactions and comments to the loop of their creative processes.

STEM Education

STEM—science, technology, engineering, and mathematics—is an acronym used in schools and institutions of higher education to discuss the need for skills in the workforce that enable individuals to work with technologies and develop new ones. The United States, for instance, would like to enhance the STEM skills of its college graduates so that they are more employable and can contribute to the country's future economic prosperity. Makerspaces have a focus on many of these same skills, and they can be a practical means of putting the theory of the classroom to work.

Maker Culture—Share Your Stuff!

The maker movement or maker culture (covered in detail in chapter 2) incorporates some of the shared knowledge–shared tool ethic discussed already. However, people who are engaged in making are also committed to sharing the designs that they used to create their products and projects. Having an open design culture means that Maker A can save time in her or his process by finding one or more models to guide the creation. She or he can also share ending project designs with Makers B and C and so on, thereby inspiring further making. The additive impacts of this openness are amazing, as we shall see.

Making Products in Makerspaces

Makerspaces in libraries can be used to make all sorts of things. There is deeper coverage of this topic in the chapters ahead, but table 1.1 is a list of the most common tools or creation options available in library makerspaces, from an informal 2013 survey of 109 library makerspaces (see the appendix for details).

Table 1.1. The 15 Most Common Technologies and Activities in Library Makerspaces ($n = 109$)

TECHNOLOGY/ACTIVITY	LIBRARIES	
	n	%
Computer workstations	73	67
3D printing	50	46
Photo editing	49	45
Video editing	47	43
Computer programming/software	43	39
Art and crafts	40	37
Scanning photos to digital	39	36
Creating a website or online portfolio	37	34
Digital music recording	36	33
3D modeling	34	31
Arduino/Raspberry Pi	33	30
Other	33	30
Animation	31	28
High-quality scanner	31	28
Tinkering	28	26

Starting a Makerspace

So, to recap, wherever making happens is a makerspace. This loose definition means that a flexible approach can be taken to budgeting for and developing one. A makerspace might be a large room filled with thousands of dollars of 3D printers and digital fabrication machines along with high-end computers, scanners, and other equipment. This might cost tens of thousands of dollars, not including the room in which, or the furniture upon which, the devices reside. It might be a small collection of tools hung up on a wall in a meeting room or at one end of a library building, perhaps with a table dedicated for making activities. This might be more of a few hundred dollars to start, adding raw materials here and there over time.

Details on planning and budgeting are in chapter 5, but you must have four things to create a makerspace. First, your community has to have an interest in a makerspace: someone has to want to use it. Second, there has to be time available for someone in the library to heed the interest of the community and organize a response to it. Third, there has to be space available in the library to host maker activities, whether it is space shared with multiple activities or a dedicated room. Finally, there needs to be financial resources available—whether from grants, the library budget, or donations—to purchase equipment and supplies and to increase the available space, staff time, and interest (through marketing).

⊚ Creating and Collaborating in Libraries

As noted earlier, libraries serve people in a variety of ways, which include giving them a place to create and a place to talk. Yes, Ray Bradbury wrote *Fahrenheit 451* in the University of California, Los Angeles, library. We can point to countless examples of writers and scholars working on books and other publications at a table in a library. It is also true that much exchange of information comes through publications that often have some tie to the library; that is, authors do a lot of research in libraries, using library resources. Furthermore, books, DVDs, and other library items inspire a lot of people to study, create, invent, discover, and chronicle exciting things.

Makerspaces extend this capacity of sharing space and knowledge by increasing the types of work that can happen in a library. Now library patrons can see physical items appear from their labors rather than just words on a page. They can work with tools that take them from reading about robots to seeing them scoot across the floor. Patrons can hold the skull of a snake in their hands fresh from the 3D printer. They can also move from primarily consuming information in the library to making physical and virtual things there. A new world of creation awaits!

⊚ Key Points

- Makerspaces are a combination of tools, an interested community of users, and a mind-set that provides for participants to teach one another and share their creations and ideas with the world.
- Makerspaces combine the characteristics of shared knowledge and tools with a focus on hands-on learning and exploration, a desire to cowork on projects alongside other makers, an attention to STEM education, and a dedication to the maker culture's ethos of sharing what is made with others.
- Makerspaces represent an intriguing opportunity for libraries to extend their mission of sharing resources with the widest audience possible to expand access and encourage learning.

⊚ References

Cavalcanti, Gui. 2013. "Is It a Hackerspace, Makerspace, TechShop, or FabLab?" *Make:*. http://makezine.com/2013/05/22/the-difference-between-hackerspaces-makerspaces-tech shops-and-fablabs/.

Levy, Steven. 2010. *Hackers: Heroes of the Computer Revolution*. Sebastopol, CA: O'Reilly Media.

Makerspace.com. 2013. "What's a Makerspace?" http://makerspace.com/home-page.

CHAPTER 2

The Maker Movement and Building Up a Making Mind-Set

TO UNDERSTAND WHERE THE DRIVE TO LOCATE MAKING in libraries comes from, it is important to review the history of making. This might seem like a silly premise in that people have always been making: making stuff is part of the nature of humanity. The outcome of modern making is all around us, just as there are examples of historical making in houses and buildings just down the street as well as that collected in museums and preserved at historical sites. But it is worth investigating where this new recent desire to make and create comes from. As will become clear, making today is in the process of being transformed by technology into something different from the making that existed before.

◎ Making as It Was

All making used to be really hard to do well. The process of coming up with an idea for a product, designing its form, imagining a method to create it, gathering materials and tools, and finally ending up with a finished product used to take a lot of time. The only way to make the process more efficient was to focus on a particular area of creation (e.g., blacksmithing, sewing, carpentry) and work at it over time to gain experience. This is not to say that all making in the past represented fine craftship or was taken on only by specialists. Lots of needs were met over the centuries by people improvising solutions to situations to survive, whether in repairing structures, stitching fabric into clothing, or creating containers for food. Anyone could complete these same actions today with the same amount of skill and resources that their ancestors had, but imagine going the next step.

To produce something intricate, involved, and useful required great talent and the right tools. That talent could be gained only by a craftsperson working many years to learn the ins and outs of the trade. The tools could be hard to find. The slow pace of gaining skills made it difficult for innovative ideas to be brought to reality until the process could be learned. Practice and the right process led to the regular creation of items such as clocks, shoes, jewelry, and even foodstuffs such as grains. Once everything was in place, it could work well.

◎ Making as It Has Been

Starting in the late eighteenth century, the development of machinery allowed for greater volumes of products to be produced without the individual toil of multiple craftspeople. The factories that arose in the nineteenth century during the Industrial Revolution combined the activities of various crafts into a single location dedicated to turning raw materials into finished products. By using machinery and concentrating multiple talented individuals in one place, it was easier to turn out large numbers of products and have a creative team fine-tune products and invent new ones. Eventually, trained operators could run machinery to churn out products of a quality and regularity that craftspersons of a century earlier could not have produced on their best day. The factory was typically owned by a small group of people who decided what it would produce and who employed dozens or hundreds of workers to make it happen.

This is effectively the world that we live in today. The products that society demands are designed, tested, focus-grouped, built, manufactured, and sold by a combination of businesses. Entry into this world of creators is relatively difficult without the capital to purchase or access equipment and machinery. It is also a mechanism for producing many of a product rather than unique one-off items, although levels of customization are possible in many product industries. For many individuals who have innovative or interesting ideas, the requirements for knowledge, tools, and the money to bring them together are far too difficult.

◎ Making as It Is Becoming

But what if something could be made without the maker knowing much about the process of creating that item? What if you could turn to groups of people, online and in person, who would share ideas and collaborate with you? What if an item could be produced without a factory full of expensive, specialized equipment? Or what if a product's design could be found online, modified, prototyped, and sent out for production or produced close at hand? These are three striking aspects of the combination of digital tools and digital sharing to the process of making (Anderson 2012). Perhaps the dynamic of making and creation is not something restricted to the relatively few individuals who can combine their desire to create with a team of designers and a factory full of tools.

The Maker Movement

The surge of interest in creating physical items with digital tools and Internet-shared plans and techniques is known as the *maker movement*. Some aspects of the maker movement have been with us for a long time in the form of home hobbyists, arts and crafts groups, shop classes, practical education, and science fairs. Around 2005, when *Make:* magazine began publishing reports on different kinds of making and interesting projects to make, this activity was identified as an ongoing area of interest for a growing group of people. The publisher's creation of a nationwide series of "maker faires" further created venues for makers to express themselves (Anderson 2013). See figure 2.1 for a look inside a maker faire. The movement was born, at least as a collective concept.

One thing that has changed the process of making from isolated, individual, small, or focused group efforts has been the impact of collaboration among makers, often in a single space. It can be a group of people working on individual iterations of a similar type of project, or it can be individual artisans working with diverse media. The idea of coworking is one in which two or more individuals are working in the same physical space. They

Figure 2.1. Maker Faire 2012. Day 2. *Image provided through a CC BY 2.0 License by the New York Hall of Science, http://www.flickr.com/photos/nysci/8048617340*

may be working on the same large project or on two or more different projects, but they can turn to one another for advice and suggestions. This mode of work is drawn from the example of hackerspaces mentioned in chapter 1 where programmers would gather in one space to share ideas and collaborate on projects. In the makerspace, there is enough space for work on design and physical creation using multiple types of media side by side. The paper artist and the metal sculptor can work alongside the programmer and the person crafting electronic devices.

The makerspace model was also heavily influenced by the creation of fab labs, led by Neil Gershenfeld of MIT's Center for Bits and Atoms. These labs, dedicated to the fabrication of items, consist of digital equipment for designing products and the digitally driven tools to create them (including laser cutters and computerized numerical control equipment). The concept caught on and has been replicated through the creation of hundreds of fab labs around the world, all of which operate with a common minimum equipment requirement and a shared mission. They were initially created for the rapid prototyping of products by local entrepreneurs, providing services not readily available in many parts of the world. They are also open to the general public and, while not centrally owned, must remain open to sharing ideas and activities with other fab labs.

Alongside and within the coworking and collaboration is a willingness to teach others. Makers who share space do not necessarily share an equivalence of talent. People come to the makerspace with a love for the creation of items and an acceptance of makers who may not know as much as they do. The environment is typically one of shared equipment and shared talents put to work on individual and shared creations. Perhaps it is better to frame this in terms of the people who come to the makerspace for the first time. What do they expect? They want to be inspired by the culture of making that pervades the space. They want to be able to use equipment or other tools that they cannot afford themselves. They want to learn new techniques to do what they love from those in the makerspace. They want to perhaps have their creations shaped by someone working in a completely different medium—perhaps a medium they might turn to themselves. This all requires a positive community environment.

Community is the defining element of the maker movement on both a local and international scale. Individuals have to have a reason to cowork, something that motivates them to collaborate and share space. There is more coverage of ways to organize and select making oeuvres later in the book, but accept for now that makers are going to network only if they feel acceptance and a sense of peer bonding. This allows for the tremendous collaboration and training alluded to earlier. Now, imagine this taking place on a larger scale, with interconnections among smaller maker communities enabled by the Internet (Dougherty 2012). Designs for products can be shared online or modified in collaboration with makers across the globe. How-to videos can be created and accessed by a much wider audience. Podcasts and video conferencing tools bring makers together in ways never possible before.

Making and Learning

In addition to the community focus of the maker movement, there is thought to be an educational impact that a person can gain from the act of making. There is an allusion in the description of making that connects the movement to education: that the community provides an instructional role for makers to learn from other makers. The effect of the act of making on learning can be further developed. Dougherty (2013) offers a lengthy list of possibilities for doing so that are being pursued and that can use more hands to make them happen. They include teaching students the maker mind-set, creating best practices in teaching making, and building makerspaces in a variety of community contexts, among others. There is an expectation that the act of creating something teaches not only practical skills (beyond the theory of reading about a process) but gives enactors a visual context to apply to future creations and innovations. What is made may not matter at all; it can still influence the thought process, vision, and ability to connect of a learning maker. These abilities can enhance a person's thinking and work in many different fields.

Participatory Culture

The first educational application of making relates to Henry Jenkins's concept of participatory culture. Jenkins imagined a culture in which people were not only the passive consumers of media but also the creators of media (Jenkins 2009). For instance, we can see this idea in practice with YouTube. People watch commercially produced music videos, instructional videos, and episodes of television dramas, but they can also create their own videos and upload them. The same experience applies to a variety of Internet sites and mobile device apps in the creation and sharing of images, text, and video online by the many as they also experience the more polished creations of the few. This idea of being a participant and creator has extended to areas beyond media. If applied to a wider view of the ways that human beings consume products, a similar move to self-creation or self-fabrication can be seen in the maker movement.

Learning is more than a by-product of self-fabrication. By putting the means of forming and shaping items into the hands of students, teachers allow for independent progress on building tasks. The benefits of spontaneous collaboration on projects can further put students in the role of teacher, giving them opportunities to examine and explain their practices. All of this imparts more understanding to students. At the very least, the freedom to participate in creation (whether digital or physical) puts tools in the hands of learners, which that they can utilize beyond their immediate tasks.

Constructionism

The second application of making to education comes from the theory of constructionism, pioneered by Seymour Papert. Constructionism posits that while learners create mental models to help them learn, actually creating a meaningful product strengthens their learning. Seeing that product or the process of creating the product reveal a concept reinforces the student's understanding of that concept. This is often accomplished by the use of problem-based learning exercises in which the student is given a problem to overcome that will teach her or him about the subject being covered (Stager 2013).

Problems are very much an expected part of maker activities. The driving force of most maker projects is a desire to solve one or more problems while creating an object. It seems like a natural fit to devise maker activities that teach or reinforce lessons for students to learn. One example of how constructionism has directly influenced makers and makerspaces is that there are a number of programming languages used in makerspace workshops, including Scratch and Logo, that were designed with constructionist principles in mind (Martinez and Stager 2013).

The Drive for STEM Experiences

For several years, there has been an interest expressed in education to increase content and study of science, technology, engineering, and mathematics, otherwise known as STEM. Whether tied to increasing national competitiveness, filling open positions in high-technology fields, or broadening the intellectual capacities of students, the need for increased STEM learning opportunities has been a focus of educational efforts. Increased exposure to content in these fields has been the prescription, and the makers of the world are ready with projects, tools, and teaching aplenty to work on this problem (Honey and Siegel 2011). While there is some discussion on whether there is really a gap or lack of STEM-ready graduates to fill needed positions, increased education in these areas does not appear to have a downside. Finding ways to connect students with existing makerspaces or finding opportunities to add maker activities into the curriculum (perhaps into libraries) will help increase STEM exposure. Some young makers might even find themselves employed by large manufacturers due to their early interest in making (Harris 2013). See figure 2.2 for a STEM learning program.

There is a related drive not only to improve students' abilities in science and mathematics but to involve the arts in this process. Adding the word *arts* to STEM creates something called STEAM, which adds to the acronym exposure to the performing and visual arts. The idea is that students gain skills from music, art, dance, and other arts complementary to those built within the traditionally linked science and math. The arts are thought to be effective in holdings students' attention while aiding in the development of their cognitive skills. The creativity often associated with the arts can have applications in other types of creation (Sousa and Pilecki 2013). This approach is even more fitting to the breadth of creativity available in many makerspaces, where engineering and artistic creations can exist side by side as well as integrated efforts.

Figure 2.2. Army supports STEM and Beyond Night. *Image provided through a CC BY 2.0 License by U.S. Army RDECOM, http://www.flickr.com/photos/rdecom/8518139625*

ⓖ Making as It Can Be

What does the future hold for making? The personal fabricators that Neil Gershenfeld (2005) imagines as a part of any household, making any needed product, may still be a few years away. In the meantime, the growth of affordable computer-driven sewing and cutting machines alongside 3D printers and scanners points toward a much more flexible and open world of making. Putting high-quality creation tools in the hands of a wider group of people could lead to greater variety in products, whether made for individuals or leading to the creation of new smaller brands in several industries. Open-source sharing of designs can make it easier for new makers to get into the market. Beyond designs, a number of maker equipment manufacturers are planning to operate under open patents that would keep plans for their equipment available to the community, even if bought out by a larger company (Dean 2012). Will this lead to a more diversified marketplace composed of many small makers competing with large manufacturers across the web? Can it be a so-called Third Industrial Revolution (Anderson 2012, 41) that applies our information and knowledge economy to the creation of physical materials? That is the potential of the maker movement.

ⓖ The Maker Mind-Set and Libraries: Why Do This?

So what makes librarians think that they should be involved with making? In an informal 2013 survey of librarians who either have or are planning to have a makerspace (see the appendix for details), respondents were asked, "When people ask you why you have a makerspace, what do you tell them?" Here is how a few of them responded:

- "We think the makerspace will fit into our core mission to support the research, teaching, and coursework of our students, faculty, and staff. We are enabling patrons to extend the application of their knowledge in order to manifest their ideas, learning, and research."
- "So there is a free community spot to create and get to know other community members. To share expertise and learn from one another."
- "Not only do we continue to do the important work of preservation and access as we have done all along, but increasingly there is an expectation that libraries will support content creation. Without giving patrons access to the newly-available tools of content creation so they can experiment with them, how can we know what's possible and what directions they'll want to go in?"
- "I say that the whole library is a makerspace, we just make scholarship."

These librarians, along with many others, are opening up their libraries to makerspaces (Gutsche 2013). They have taken on the task of supporting the technologies, projects, and workshops that fit their communities. They recognize that the library is a shared space for schools, communities, and campuses where anyone and everyone can come together (Watters 2013). They are effectively broadening their mind-sets to include the creation of items because of these essential points:

- Making is in keeping with the library's mission to provide access to resources and technologies.

- The library is already a makerspace, based on the activities going on within the library.
- The library gives community members a place to come together and support one another's creations.
- The library can support educational efforts in STEM and other areas through hosting a makerspace.

These statements can be turned into questions for any library: Do these points fit your library setting? Could they if you reexamined your library's role? Continue reading to see how libraries have begun implementing makerspaces.

Key Points

- Making is a constant but evolving human endeavor.
- The maker movement arose to combine digital tools and open-source sharing to create physical and digital objects.
- Makerspaces can affect education by increasing exposure to STEM and STEAM concepts and activities.

References

Anderson, Chris. 2012. *Makers: The New Industrial Revolution*. London: Random House Business Books.
———. 2013. "Maker Movement." *Wired* 21 (5): 106.
Dean, Alexandra. 2012. "The DIY Movement Meets the VCs." *Bloomberg Businessweek* 4267: 55–56.
Dougherty, Dale. 2012. "The Maker Movement." *Innovations: Technology, Governance, Globalization* 7 (3): 11–14.
———. 2013. "The Maker Mindset." In *Design, Make, Play: Growing the Next Generation of STEM Innovators*, edited by Margaret Honey and David Kanter, 7–11. New York: Routledge.
Gershenfeld, Neil A. 2005. *Fab: The Coming Revolution on Your Desktop—From Personal Computers to Personal Fabrication*. New York: Basic Books.
Gutsche, Betha. 2013. "Makerspaces in Libraries: Patron's Delight, Staff's Dread?" *Alki* 29 (1): 28–30.
Harris, Stephen. 2013. "Why Manufacturers Should Embrace the Maker Movement." *Engineer* 2. Online.
Honey, Margaret, and Eric Siegel. 2011. "The Maker Movement." *Education Week* 30 (19): 32–25.
Jenkins, Henry. 2009. *Confronting the Challenges of Participatory Culture: Media Education for the 21st Century*. Cambridge, MA: MIT Press.
Martinez, Sylvia Libow, and Gary Stager. 2013. *Invent to Learn: Making, Tinkering, and Engineering in the Classroom*. Torrance, CA: Constructing Modern Knowledge Press.
Sousa, David A., and Thomas Pilecki. 2013. *From STEM to STEAM: Using Brain-Compatible Strategies to Integrate the Arts*. Thousand Oaks, CA: Corwin Press.
Stager, G. S. 2013. "Papert's Prison Fab Lab: Implications for the Maker Movement and Education Design." In *Proceedings of the 12th International Conference on Interaction Design and Children*, 487–90. New York: ACM.
Watters, Audrey. 2013. "The Case for a Campus Makerspace." *Hack Education* (blog). February 6. http://hackeducation.com/2013/02/06/the-case-for-a-campus-makerspace/.

CHAPTER 3

An Overview of Makerspace Implementations

SO HOW CAN LIBRARIANS BRING THE MAKER MOVEMENT into their libraries through the creation of makerspaces and the encouragement of maker activities? Many libraries are already equipped with space, programming, and tools that provide opportunities for making. The place to start with this question is to consider how libraries can make these opportunities an intentional and organized part of their service offerings. As this book demonstrates, there are many ways to make a makerspace happen.

Makerspaces exist as communities that exemplify the qualities examined in chapter 2: coworking, collaboration, teaching and learning, open sharing of ideas. The best result comes from a combination that brings together community, activity making, and the library's mission.

◎ Surveying Library Makerspaces

To get a sense of what makerspaces in libraries look like, an informal survey was conducted in 2013 that had 143 respondents (see the appendix for details). Of that total, 109 librarians responded affirmatively, with 58 respondents (53 percent) saying that they have a makerspace or similar space in place and with 51 (47 percent) saying that they plan to add a makerspace. An additional 34 librarians responded that they did not have a makerspace nor did they plan to add one, but those responses eliminated them from being included in the questions that followed.

Makerspaces appear in most types of libraries: 55 (51 percent) of the respondents are in public libraries, 38 (36 percent) in academic libraries, and 10 (9 percent) in school libraries. The remaining 4 (4 percent) chose *other* for their type of library, representing combinations of school and public libraries (n = 2), a community college library, and a graduate school for information science, while none selected the option of special libraries.

Library makerspaces are found throughout the United States and around the world and are overwhelmingly recent additions to their libraries. Libraries in 30 states responded to the survey, along with 7 countries: Australia, Canada, China, Denmark, Japan, Netherlands, and United Kingdom. In terms of their longevity, 46 respondents (46 percent) noted that their makerspaces had been in place for less than 1 year, 13 (13 percent) for 1–2 years, 5 (5 percent) for 2–3 years, 2 (2 percent) for 3–4 years, and 4 (4 percent) for more than 4 years. Librarians who had not yet implemented a makerspace made up 29 (29 percent) of the responses with *other* as their response.

Naming a makerspace was an interesting process for the librarians who responded. From the survey, 73 of the 109 makerspaces (67 percent) have been named in some way or are located in existing digital creation spaces with their own names. The word *make* was very popular in the names, with 31 named spaces including the word in their names in some form and with 19 of those spaces clearly identified as a *makerspace*. *Library* was also popular, with 19 spaces including the word as part of their names. Other popular terms include *space* (23 makerspaces), *media* (15), *lab* (14), variations on *create* (*creative*, *creation*, etc.) (10), and *digital* (8). So, one approach might be to combine all these words for a clearly top-of-the-line makerspace. For instance, the "Digital Media Creation Maker Lab Space" has a nice ring to it, doesn't it? Seriously, though, it is interesting to see the use percentage of terms to learn how makerspaces are being positioned in the communities in which they exist. Also, it is good to know at once that *makerspace* is a recognizable enough term to name a space after, while it is clear that other variations seem to work well, too. A Wordle showing the repetition of terms used in the names is included in figure 3.1.

Figure 3.1. What's your name? Terms used to describe makerspaces.

⑥ Forming Your Makerspace

Makerspaces as a whole reflect multiple histories of creation and various plans for operation. Several approaches have been used to form them in libraries. Travis Good (2013) outlined three of them:

Collaborate

The library works with an existing makerspace or makers group in the community to bring making activities into the library. The case example provided involves a public library partnered with a local makers group to locate a 50-foot trailer filled with equipment near the library for library patrons to use. This approach can, among other things, lessen the support role required of library staff members (Belbin and Newcombe 2012). It can also call on the library to be willing to give up some control over the resulting space (Kenney 2013).

Centralize, Develop, Deploy

In a larger library system, a makerspace can be established in the main library or a single branch to try out projects and workshops before making activities are launched in other locations. The profiled library, a large metropolitan public library, uses a central makerspace at its main library to try out technologies and resources and develop staff skills, all of which can then be spread out to its wider community through branch libraries.

Opportunistic/Entrepreneurial

The library commits to having a makerspace and then finds ways to repurpose existing resources (space, furniture, equipment, etc.) and funding to fulfill the commitment. In the academic science and engineering library in Good's (2013) article, expenditures on Arduino kits (small microcontrollers; more on these in chapter 8), whiteboard paint, and 3D printers were justified by comparisons to more expensive expenditures on journals, books, and other library purchases. It was also able to add equipment through an internal grant.

In reviewing makerspaces in the literature and in the makerspace profiles in this book, several makerspace origin stories fit with one of these three approaches. Partnering with an existing group of makers can bring expertise to the programs and activities that the library makerspace offers, and it can help the library begin making things without having to start from scratch. Having the chance to fine-tune technology and project offerings in one location before rolling them out elsewhere can make sense in a larger library system, in a loose consortium of libraries, or in the multiple libraries in a school district. Many libraries will find themselves in the place of having to convert existing funds, space, and resources to create a makerspace.

Libraries might use other approaches beyond these three, though. The following allow alternative entry points that might work better for other libraries.

Recognize the Makerspace within Your Library

This is not as simplistic a suggestion as it might first appear. You cannot simply call a library a makerspace and then it becomes so. But you can look at your library with new eyes and identify existing activities, services, and technologies that are already providing making experiences for library patrons. For instance, your academic library might check out microphones and cameras to students for video projects. Or your school library computers may be used by students to play Minecraft after their required assignments are completed. Or your public library might host knitting groups or have craft sessions as part of its summer reading program. These are maker activities, and while they may not be all that you want to offer or everything that your community would like to make in the library, they do provide you with some maker cred: a foundation for what could be. You can recognize that you have a makerspace already and declare that your library is one.

The Slow Build

Jump into the creation of a makerspace, but do not add everything right away. There is no set of required services, technologies, or operations that you must have to get started—no top-10 list to check off or you can't use the name. Add something—either in response to the wishes expressed by your library users or to spark some creativity and get people thinking—then you can build from there. And there should be no reluctance to move into maker mode, give the potentially positive impact that it can have on your community. Martinez and Stager (2013) assure educators that "you are better prepared than you think" to take on maker activities, noting the many digital means for individuals to write, make videos, and find other ways to tell their stories. Entry points for these activities may be free websites and apps accessed from library computers or patron cell phones, and they can be scaled upward with the addition of inexpensive microphones and purchased software. Beginning with these tools or whatever you decide to start with, the makerspace can grow over time.

Start Big

The direct opposite of the slow build is to build a space that will accommodate many types of making at once. Having enough funding to do so is essential to make this happen, but it also requires a different mind-set to the more gradual nature of some of the earlier approaches. Starting off with a dedicated space and a lot of equipment is a way to stay ahead of ongoing demands for new capacities from your makers and to encourage interplay to happen among different making technologies. It is setting off with the expectation that you will have multiple making projects going on simultaneously. You might choose to do this because your goals for a makerspace are bigger than just introducing a few maker activities. Perhaps you are also trying to meet various kinds of maker needs, from engineering students creating prototypes of products to people experimenting with Arduino kits and groups taking photography classes. Woodbury and Charnas (2013) share the details of the think[box] innovation center at Case Western Reserve University, which is currently a 3,000-square-foot makerspace with $1 million in equipment that will soon transition into a 50,000-square-foot, seven-story building. That is far bigger than what most makerspaces will ever be, but it provides an upper end of the scale example of building big. If you hope to inspire your community with your makerspace, starting big will introduce many opportunities at once and can lead to cross-pollination of creativity. Again, the money and a concrete plan have to be in place to pull this off (more on these considerations in chapters 4 and 5).

Do It by the Book

An approach that can work as a stand-alone method or in cooperation with the other approaches is to find a model makerspace that you would like to emulate, see what it has, and follow its plan (either entirely or in part). This could work with a model that is either a large space or a small space. The draw of this approach is that you are avoiding re-creating the wheel and are outfitting your space in a manner that works. You are starting with a design that may have taken the other makerspace years to build and, in doing so, saving yourself that time. A caution with this approach is to not merely try to replicate the model space but to adapt it to fit your community's needs and interests. A couple of sites that can be helpful to use as plans or that point to sample plans are from YOUmedia Network ("Getting Started," 2013) and the "Makerspace Playbook" (Makerspace.com 2013).

⊚ Engaging Your Community

No matter which of these approaches appeals to you, something that cannot be forgotten is the community in which your library operates. The most incredible library makerspace is not a creation unto itself; it needs to reflect the interests of the library's community. Suggestions on gauging and building interest come in chapter 4, but it is crucial to understand that if makerspaces are all about making, there have to be makers who come to the space. An underutilized room of expensive equipment is not the outcome that you are looking for as you follow these approaches. The first task is for librarians to recognize that this service can be a part of their libraries and this work a part of their job descriptions (Britton 2012). The Maker Jawn Initiative at the Free Library of Philadelphia stresses the importance of engaging as many library staff members as possible to create a support network for patrons and one another (Tait and Steele 2014). The second and even more important task is to see where a makerspace can serve the community.

◎ Creating Interest vs. Overwhelming

One caution that can be offered to makerspaces is to be neither too large nor too small. While this sounds like most of Polonius's equivocating advice to his son Laertes in Shakespeare's *Hamlet* ("Neither a borrower nor a lender be"), there is a useful lesson here. The goal of the library makerspace is to meet existing community needs for creative experiences while trying to motivate the rest of the community to create. Imagine your community as populating a dartboard. Those in the bull's-eye are the people whom you have solidly in mind as you are planning your space and who are (hopefully) giving input on the planning. As you move further out in the rings of the board, each border that you cross is populated by people who will need higher amounts of convincing that the makerspace is for them.

While you may never interest people at the farther reaches, you have to find the right balance of offerings to keep the committed group interested and returning while not scaring off potential users. Now, what might scare them off? It could be that your makerspace has too much high-tech equipment and looks like it is a place for engineers only. Your space could have just a couple of items to start with and not encourage people to inquire for more, or your makerspace might be too focused on artistic creation, for instance, and not attract someone who might be interested in robotics. Now, not every makerspace is going to serve the entire community of the library, nor is every makerspace trying to reach the most reluctant members of the community. But as you are trying to get started and create interest, you should have the preponderance of your offerings match what you know will be used, but you should still have something on hand that will make people curious and draw them in (e.g., a 3D printer, soldering irons, examples of completed projects).

◎ Programming vs. Open Labs

One distinction to make in planning makerspaces is whether the library will provide dedicated space to use for maker activities or will instead offer programming on maker technologies and topics. Or will it offer both? This may be a question that changes over the lifetime of your makerspace. You might hold occasional workshops or a monthly series of programs to start off your efforts and then move to offering open hours in a makerspace in the library. Or your library setting might not lend itself to holding public programs and instead might find making activities linked to specific class needs. Perhaps that would evolve into open, creative periods with your maker activities. Yet another possibility is that your maker operations are always mobile, moving from site to site in your community, without opening an actual space. This is a consideration that should definitely go into the planning for the space. Chapter 11 discusses programming ideas and ways to balance these two approaches.

◎ Getting Dirty in Your Making

While making takes various forms and has various requirements, one element that is discussed among makers is clean vs. dirty spaces. Many maker activities are relatively clean: computer programming, sewing, LEGO robotics, green screen videography, even most 3D printing. They probably will not threaten most library furnishings or carpet with damage or stains. Yet, soldering, woodworking, computerized numerical control cutting machines, cooking, and ceramics might make a mess. They might also smell bad, make a lot of noise, or create fumes that need to be vented out of the building. It is crucial for the impact of the making to be considered, on those in the makerspace and for patrons in the rest of the library. This includes the annoyance factor as well as safety considerations. The environment available in the library may guide the choices of making that can occur there. At the very least, you have to imagine what the makerspace will look like if everything you envisage happening there is actually going on. If dirty space is not available or cannot be planned for in the initial launch of the space, it can always be added in later.

⊚ Considering Different Library Types

In addition to the approaches and issues addressed so far, others might affect your library depending on your setting. Although many maker activities are going to be fairly identical in implementation regardless of the setting, particular areas of focus can come into play. Separating these library types out briefly should not overshadow the potential for multitype library partnership efforts for making either.

Public Libraries

Can public libraries continue to carry on their mission of providing information access to the public by adding access to creative equipment? Some argue that it is a logical step for public libraries to add making activities to their repertoire (Torrone 2011). Otherwise, many members of the public might not have access to fabrication equipment. Public libraries have the broadest population to reach and can target makerspace activities to specific groups and the community at large. Teens and children's activities can be the focus of a defined makerspace area or mobile maker programming. Adults can also have opportunities to create. Patrons may wish to create artwork, learn how to design products, or collaborate on efforts that lead to small businesses. Local businesses may also be able to use library software and equipment to help with their own products, given that they may not have made the investment in this equipment on their own (Cash 2011). Here is another opportunity for the multiplying impact of the public library's purchases to be felt in the community: the library makes the purchase, and several individuals and organizations can benefit. There are many possible groups to market to, and depending on the interest shown by the community, it can be difficult to meet everyone's needs.

Academic Libraries

On college and university campuses, makerspaces may be the realm of engineering, design, and science students practicing the talents that they will apply in industry upon graduation. They may also be aimed at a wider audience of students working on projects, from creating art to visualizing anatomy to recording oral history (Woodbury and Charnas 2013). The academic environment provides many opportunities for maker equipment and activities to have a direct tie to learning. One question that might occur is why teaching and research departments do not just add their own makerspaces. Some may have them already, but these spaces tend to not match the number of hours that the library can be open. This is often a capacity of the academic library that makes it a perfect place for the makerspace.

School Libraries

School library makerspaces are generally geared toward adding hands-on interaction to the school setting. The school day and curricular demands are tight on time, and maker activities are often added only when they clearly add to students' potential for learning. There are many making activities that can meet this criterion, and that makes the makerspace a viable component for schools and school libraries. It is also possible, once a makerspace is equipped in the school library, to use open periods and after-school times to let students stay engaged inventing, creating, and building their skills. Gustafson (2013) articulates how work in a makerspace can meet several of the American Association of School Libraries' standards for 21st-century learners.

To help visualize implementing makerspaces in these three settings, take a look at the three makerspace profiles that follow.

⑥ Library Makerspace Profile: Richland Public Library, Columbia, SC

http://www.richlandlibrary.com/check-it-out/teens

Christina Fuller-Gregory, Teen Services Librarian

How Did It Start?

The library staff learned that 14.6 percent of the population in Columbia were teens. They did not have a set space for teens, and they wanted to have a way for teens to bridge from the library's children's space (as they age out) and move into being adult customers. Fuller-Gregory had read a lot about HoMaGo ("hanging out, messing around, geeking out") and wanted to have a space where teens could do all three. The teen space came out of these thoughts. The library staff started looking at other "dream" teen centers, and this gave them an idea of where to go. They already had the go-ahead from their administration to start making a wish list.

What Does It Include?

- Two Makerbot 3D printers (in constant use)
- Flip cameras
- Whisper Room—a recording booth
- Two Macs and four desktop PCs
- iPads and Surface tablets (for use in the Teen Center and the makerspace)
- Art and craft materials
- Wall talkers—dry erase walls that have been hugely popular (teens use them for Sudoku, etc.)
- Gaming (WiiU and Xbox)

How Did You Build It?

Fuller-Gregory said that it was so helpful to see technologies in use before actually adopting them. As the team visited other libraries and makerspaces, they made note of items that they would like to add. For instance, they saw a green screen in a makerspace and decided that they really wanted one. They then edited a wish list of items down into a list of things that they felt were essential and could fit into their budget. Sadly, the green screen did not make the final list. Overall, they have had great support from their administration to fund the makerspace and keep it operating.

Who Uses It?

Their focus is on teens, and they maintain an age limit of 12 to 18 years for the area. They offer structured programming, "STEAM-powered," and other things, depending on need—for example, working on Adobe Illustrator. Teens' ideas were integral to adding arts programming and technology to the space. Teens like the iPads more and have been very vocal about having access to them. Most recently, Fuller-Gregory and fellow librarian Mary Kate Quillivan have created My World, a YouTube-based learning platform that uses social media and content creation with the purpose of teaching teens video editing and filming. Teens come together for Draw My Life programs and to learn the basics of filming and editing. Content is created by teens and shared with the world via a library YouTube channel.

How Do You Market the Makerspace?

The marketing team at the library has done a great job. School outreach has been tremendously effective. Librarians showed students how to make an iPhone case with a 3D printer. When the staff visit the schools, they are not just visiting libraries but specific classes; English teachers have been a huge help in marketing. The staff held an open house for teachers to show them the equipment. They have been featured in the state's biggest newspaper and on the television news, and they were the first library in the state with a makerspace for teens.

How Do You Support It?

The library has three librarians and two library associates to staff the space. They have created partnerships with groups in the community that provide mentoring to teens in the space. For instance, two theater companies come in and give film classes. IT-oLogy, a technology company in Columbia, has also been helpful at providing support.

How Do You Stay Aware of Developments in Makerspaces?

Fuller-Gregory is always watching out for new technology. The library is looking for low-tech ways to stay exciting, which has led staff to reach into the arts and pursue upcycling as programming ideas. They are just starting with upcycling, which is recycling waste materials into something useful. They are adding sewing machines to the makerspace, which will help with fashion upcycling.

What Do You See Happening in Your Makerspace in the Next Year?

The library wants to add newer MakerBots and laser cutters. Fuller-Gregory is looking for small video cameras to add. They will start up robotics and programming as options in January 2014. Teen outreach has become a major priority, and to promote the makerspace concept, they are adding smaller 3D printers that can be used to provide teens with limited access to the main makerspace location with a firsthand look at how a 3D printer operates. The devices being added are the Simple and the Cube.

What Is Your Advice to Others Who Would Like to Create a Makerspace?

Keep things portable. Make sure that you can move things around—even within the room. The flexibility and mobility of the equipment and activities are crucial. Also, get organized about defining items as "what you want" vs. "what you need." You have to consider whether something will be a momentary trend or something that will last.

⊚ Library Makerspace Profile: Blue Valley North High School, Overland Park, KS

http://www4.bluevalleyk12.org/bvn/lmc/

Abby Cornelius, Library Media Specialist

Terri Snethen, Library Media Specialist

How Did Your Makerspace Come to Be?

The makerspace is in a school library (figure 3.2), and in a lot of libraries the focus is simply on reading. The library is well staffed, with two full-time librarians and two library paraprofessionals. They focus their program on content creation, not just reading fiction. Students are creating content for their coursework, both virtually and in print. The library earned a $10,000 prize in 2009, and thanks to that, it has scanners, headphones/microphones, and flip cameras, and it recently bought a MakerBot 3D printer (it has since purchased a second MakerBot). They have 8,000 square feet in the library and 40 computers for students, plus laptop carts that travel around the school.

The school district administration has not been supportive of the library's makerspace efforts, but the award and building administration made it possible. The school district

Figure 3.2. Makerspace at Blue Valley North High School. *Provided by Abby Cornelius*

used to be more flexible about how library funds were spent, but now funds allotted for books in the budget have to be spent on books. The community is very interested in education. Fortunately, a local educational foundation raises money and offers grants twice per year, and the library regularly applies for them. It purchased digital cameras with one of the grants and USB headphone/microphone headsets with another, but it was not able to apply for the same grant to fund its MakerBot, due to the unwillingness of its information technology department to provide support (it did not understand the need to have a 3D printer). The library was able to buy it with the award money, however, and it is hugely popular and has inspired the industrial technology district coordinator to order more for district high schools, justifying the original purchase.

Who Uses It?

Students constantly create content with their phones and computers but like to create in other ways. There is a student who likes leatherworking and who used TinkerCAD and the 3D printer to create a tool to use in his craft. Students who were studying meteorology created topographic maps of hurricanes and a tornado with debris with the 3D printer. Students in a chemistry class were studying ions and designed 3D models of molecules and then painted each element in the correct color. They used Autodesk 123D design software to create the molecule files. They had to solve problems to achieve the designs. All juniors at the school take chemistry, and all of them worked with this project, as well as some advanced sophomores. Cornelius noted that the juniors did a better job with the 3D designs than the sophomores did. The required class is a real grind for some people, but including maker activities makes it more interesting and gives them chance to learn new software, which they will have to do in later life. It has made a real-world connection for the students beyond what they are learning in chemistry.

The school does not have as many required projects that utilize audio and video technologies, but they are an option. The librarians are required to teach some library curriculum every year, even though they are not assigned students in a class setting. They design and implement library lessons and encourage teachers to bring students in. They designed a lesson for students to create a business, a product, or a service. They create a business plan and figure out costs and what they will charge (all of which adds some math to their research component). Students are given a model of a business plan and then use Smore.com to make an online flyer. Another project with which the library has helped is for a marketing class. Students are creating board games and are just starting to design game pieces that they will create on the 3D printer. The pieces might even be figurines of the students.

Content creation is not always physical, but it's still making. School libraries are not always sufficiently funded or staffed, but the ability to make things creates a lot of interest in the library among students and the general public.

How Do You Market the Makerspace?

One method they have used is to connect people with the library through the 3D printer. Four or five classes have come in for 3D projects, and every class that comes in for other purposes watches it at work. This gets those students interested in the whole making idea. The library stays open late, and it opens early for kids to work on homework, so there are some unstructured times for students to come in and see and use the making items. It also has video games and gaming stuff. All these activities are focused on making the library a space that people want to be in. It has also had parents stop in during conference periods, and school board members have been invited to see the makerspace. All of this attention opens people's minds to the possibilities of this equipment.

How Do You Stay Aware of Developments in Makerspaces?

Twitter is the primary option. The library specialists also follow *Make:* magazine and a small group of educators who are using maker technologies that Cornelius has connected with through tweeting about her own activities.

What Do You See Happening in Your Makerspace in the Next Year?

The school has a bunch of student clubs, and Cornelius hopes to do some making programs that the clubs could sponsor and to also have the clubs create stuff that they could sell as a fund-raiser. Their next exciting thing is to add a 3D scanner, which would let them re-create so many things as design files and then print them. They can also edit and change these scans and mash them up with other demands.

What Is Your Advice to Others Who Would Like to Create a Makerspace?

Your library has to be inviting to your students first. Once people show up, they will encounter all this cool stuff. Cornelius believes in setting up very few rules and letting students experience the equipment. Just having stuff out for them to mess around with can be very effective, such as thread, yarn, buttons, socks, and more. Her teaching opportunities do not always happen in the library, and in all her teaching, she shows that the library is more than just books and reading.

Look to the American Library Association for materials on promoting teen tech week and other fun weeks. She uses these to draw attention and then finds making activities that connect with students: making bookmarks with them and mirror balls out of old CDs, for example. It is important to get kids involved in making projects after school.

◎ Library Makerspace Profile: Stanley Library, Ferrum College, Ferrum, VA

http://www.ferrum.edu/academics/stanley_library/Digital_Media_Services/index.html

Heather Wilson, Systems and Emerging Technologies Librarian

How Did Your Makerspace Come to Be?

While continuing to evolve, this makerspace was created this past summer as part of the first renovation of the first floor into the 21st Century Learning Center at Stanley Library (figure 3.3). Planning began a year ago when the library director hired Wilson into a new position: systems and emerging technologies librarian. With a background in public libraries, Wilson thought of makerspaces as an important trend in emerging technol-

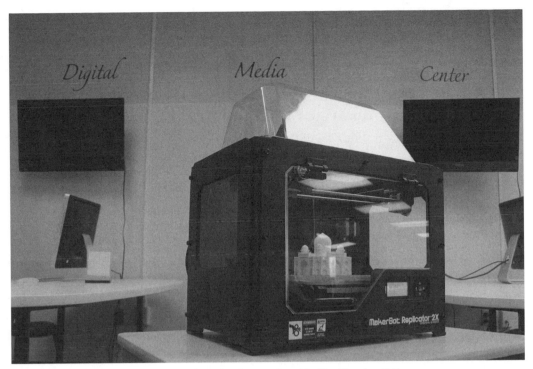

Figure 3.3. Ferrum College Digital Media Center. *Provided by Heather Wilson*

ogies. The director wanted to develop a digital media center in the library, so they started with a green screen kit, some digital cameras, and a copy of Adobe Elements software. This year, they graduated to a larger, dedicated space with multiple technology-enabled workstations and multiple licenses of Adobe Master Suite software. They then received a grant from an anonymous donor to expand digital media center services. Wilson was asked to put together a list of equipment that might be useful to add, including a 3D printer, small circuits, and a digital audio lab.

Pursuing and receiving external and internal funding has made their makerspace possible. The library director started pursuing funds and acquiring tools shortly after arriving nearly 2 years ago. Wilson believes that donors and development professionals are much more open to funding makerspaces, at least in the academic world. They are willing to donate their money to something worthy and future oriented.

How Do You Market the Makerspace?

Wilson's background is in library web design; however, that has not helped a great deal in marketing at Ferrum. There, word of mouth is far stronger. Its Facebook fans are not mostly students, so social networking has not been effective. The 3D printer does its own marketing, as does the green screen and large-format printer. She has created 3D items for display to students. Once students know that these technologies are in the library, they become very popular.

Right now, Wilson is working with her library student assistants to market their equipment and services. She will then turn toward serving student needs and assessing the makerspace activities while stepping down her marketing efforts. The makerspace is included in library tours, and she is trying to build an augmented reality tour that would show off the equipment as well. With her four student workers talking about the 3D printer and other equipment, the word is definitely getting out. Faculty members are interested in using the makerspace, as evidenced by many professors assigning video projects.

How Do You Stay Aware of Developments in Makerspaces?

Wilson finds that her job title of emerging technologies librarian gives her access to a small community of librarians to whom she can turn for advice and ideas. She has enjoyed the ability to network and participate in conferences provided by the Library and Information Technology Association and the Appalachian College Association. By and large, however, following electronic discussion groups and reading reports on the value of emerging technologies has been even more helpful. She likes to learn about what her colleagues are implementing in their libraries and then find ways to justify the addition of the technology to her director and college administrators. Once funding is secured, she can turn to a database of people who have implemented it and get further help from them. Participating in an emerging technology librarians' community on Facebook and following people on Twitter gives her a growing awareness of technologies and a resource to turn to when she needs to know more.

What Do You See Happening in Your Makerspace in the Next Year?

In the spring of 2014, the donation that the library received will make more things possible. A sound booth will be added. The 3D printer is already in Wilson's office, and she is working with it to test things out. She is now talking with her student assistants to create more ideas. Her hope is to put more technology out with the library student crew and get them working with it. She hopes to work on some small circuit projects with networking and computer science classes and perhaps include some Arduino stations and Raspberry Pi efforts. Wilson would like to see more programming opportunities available for students. In the next year, she hopes to add a laser cutter. Overall, she sees the library moving from implementing disruptive technologies to create interest to now starting to respond to demands that the technologies have created. As well, she imagines creating more educational opportunities for students and faculty to learn about the tools.

One thing that has really helped create interest in the makerspace is that there has not been technology of this sort available on campus before. Also, the college is relatively small and rural, which allows the librarians to get to know students and build activities that meet their interests. Students at Ferrum are fairly isolated and do not have opportunities for technology-enabled making within easy reach. Wilson says that it is amazing to see what students want to create. Some are interested in creating mobile apps, including some students who hunt and want to create an app to help them get permit permissions from landowners so that they and others can hunt on the property. Students from the veterinary program are interested in making animal bones with the 3D printer. Now Wilson wants to respond to these interests and find ways to meet their demands.

Finally, Wilson is intrigued by the idea that maker activities need not be in a physical space but rather as a more useful mobile operation. She hopes to move some of her programs outside the library. She believes that it is crucial to show these activities inside and outside the library. It will be interesting to see how moving technologies and maker activities out to various spaces will affect the overall usage of these items.

What Is Your Advice to Others Who Would Like to Create a Makerspace?

Wilson suggests that small academic libraries have great opportunities for making makerspaces happen in their environments due to interest from campus administrations and the availability of funding. She suggests that potential maker librarians go beyond turning to the professional literature or EDUCAUSE and find other people who have already started makerspaces. Ask them questions to get vital information on how to get the technology and how to regulate it once you have it. She learned a lot about operating a makerspace from her networking, as well as the importance of setting up policies first before you get overwhelmed.

Key Points

There are makerspaces in nearly all types of libraries in the United States and the world. There are multiple ways to approach implementing a makerspace in your library. Some key points to remember from the chapter follow:

- Making sure that the library is in tune with its community is essential to the success of the makerspace.
- Several considerations can guide librarians to find the right fit for the makerspace, including the types of programming and the types of making that will go on there.
- Public, academic, and school libraries will have specific considerations to consider when creating a makerspace.

The next chapter examines the many options available for maker technologies and making activities.

References

Belbin, Nicole, and Pat Newcombe. 2012. "Fab Labs at the Library." *Government Technology* 25 (10): 30–33.

Britton, Lauren. 2012. "A Fabulous Laboratory." *Public Libraries* 52 (4): 30–33.

Cash, Martin. 2011. "Making It . . . with a Little Help." *Winnipeg Free Press*. October 8. B6.

"Getting Started." 2013. YOUmedia Network. http://www.youmedia.org/toolkit/getting-started.

Good, Travis. 2013. "Three Makerspace Models That Work." *American Libraries* 44 (1/2): 45–47.

Gustafson, Ellen. 2013. "Meeting Needs: Makerspaces and School Libraries." *School Library Monthly* 29 (8): 35–36.

Kenney, Brian. 2013. "Meet Your Makers." *Publishers Weekly* 260 (13): 20.

Makerspace.com. 2013. "Makerspace Playbook." http://makerspace.com/wp-content/uploads/2013/02/MakerspacePlaybook-Feb2013.pdf.

Martinez, Sylvia Libow, and Gary Stager. 2013. *Invent to Learn: Making, Tinkering, and Engineering in the Classroom*. Torrance, CA: Constructing Modern Knowledge Press.

Tait, Barbara, and K-Fai Steele. 2014. "Make Jawn at the Free Library of Philadelphia: Emerging Best Practices for Maker Programming in Libraries." *Library as Incubator Project* (blog). January 27. http://www.libraryasincubatorproject.org/?p=13186.

Torrone, Phillip. 2011. "Is It Time to Rebuild & Retool Public Libraries and Make 'Tech Shops'?" *Make:*. March 3. http://makezine.com/2011/03/10/is-it-time-to-rebuild-retool-public-libraries-and-make-techshops/.

Woodbury, David, and Ian Charnas. 2013. "Fostering a Place for Invention and Creation: Two Approaches to Makerspaces on Campus." EDUCAUSE (webinar). October 28. http://www.educause.edu/library/resources/fostering-place-invention-and-creation-two-approaches-makerspaces-campus.

What Will Patrons Make in Your Makerspace?

MAKING AND MAKERSPACES CAN ENCOMPASS many different creative activities. The choices for making are many, and no makerspace can hold all of them or support every option. As flexible and mobile as makerspaces can be, there have to be some guiding principles in place to help the library support the makers in discovering their creative sides. A makerspace does not need to include every possible type of making or even be able to check off the top 10 most popular making technologies in the world among its offerings. What it does need to do is to connect with the interests and desires of its community.

As a starting point to a discussion of makerspace options, consider the results of the survey of library makerspaces (see the appendix for details). While not an all-inclusive list of every type of making included in libraries, it can be an aid to the process of imagining opportunities to offer patrons in your library. A short list of the most common maker technologies and activities is included in chapter 1, but the complete list of options is listed in table 4.1. Of the list of 55 items, all but 6 were selected by at least one maker-

Table 4.1. Technologies and Activities in Library Makerspaces ($n = 109$)

TECHNOLOGY/ACTIVITY	RESPONDENTS	
	n	%
Computer workstations	73	67
3D printing	50	46
Photo editing	49	45
Video editing	47	43
Computer programming/software	43	39
Art and crafts	40	37
Scanning photos to digital	39	36
Creating a website or online portfolio	37	34
Digital music recording	36	33
3D modeling	34	31
Arduino/Raspberry Pi	33	30
Other	33	30
Animation	31	28
High-quality scanner	31	28
Tinkering	28	26
Electronic music programming	26	24
Creating apps	24	22
Game creation	24	22
Soldering iron	24	22
Electronics	23	21
Prototyping	21	19
Robotics	19	17
Fabric shop[a]	18	17
Circuit hacking	17	16
Digital scrapbooking	16	15
Electronic book production	15	14

TECHNOLOGY/ACTIVITY	RESPONDENTS	
	n	%
Inventing	15	14
Soft circuits	15	14
VHS conversion equipment	14	13
Mobile development	13	12
Large format printer	9	8
Vinyl cutting	9	8
Laser cutting	8	7
Food/culinary arts	6	6
Screen printing	5	5
Woodworking[b]	4	4
Bicycle building/maintenance	3	3
Ceramics	3	3
Computerized numerical control machines	3	3
Jewelry making[c]	3	3
Plastics/composites	3	3
Dark room	2	2
Industrial sewing machine	2	2
Milling machine	2	2
Mold making	2	2
Automotive	1	1
Guitar repair	1	1
Potter's wheel and kiln	1	1
Silkscreening	1	1
Blacksmithing	0	0
Glass shop[d]	0	0
Letterpress	0	0
Metal shop[e]	0	0
Stained glass	0	0
Welding	0	0

[a] Sewing machines, leather sewing machines, computerized numerical control embroidery, etc.

[b] Table saw, panel saw, bandsaw, drill press, belt sanders, etc.

[c] Acetylene torch, buffing station, annealing pans, forming tools, metal smithing, etc.

[d] Glass blowing, kiln, jewelry making, etc.

[e] Metal lathe, cold saw, horizontal bandsaw, sheet metal shear, etc.

TEXTBOX 4.1.

"OTHER" TECHNOLOGIES AND
ACTIVITIES IN LIBRARY MAKERSPACES

Beading

Button maker

Comics

e-Discovery kits (engineering kits)

Film studio

Green screen

Hand tools (hammers, pliers, screwdrivers, wrenches, etc.)

Knitting and crocheting

Large monitors on the wall to attach laptops

LEGOs

littleBits

MaKey MaKey

Microscope

Oscilloscope

Papercrafts (e.g., Origami)

Presentation space with small stage

Scratch

Scrounge (for toy and scenario making)

Seismograph

Server rack and networking equipment

Snap circuits

Squishy circuits

Tool library

T-shirt heat press

Video conferencing (Skype)

Video production

Video recording equipment

Watercolor

Yarn

space (those six were welding, stained glass, metal shop activities, letterpress, glass shop activities, and blacksmithing). The items included in the list were gathered from surveys conducted to help create new library makerspaces and from technologies and activities mentioned in the makerspace literature.

Another aspect to consider from the survey results is the number of technologies in use at each makerspace. From the 109 library makerspaces represented in the survey, respondents chose technologies or activities from the list of 55 a total of 956 times. That means that the average makerspace in the survey is offering nearly 9 making options to its patrons. A few respondents listed only one technology or activity, but the majority had a list of items in the double digits. This would suggest that for most library makerspaces, making is not a one-trick operation; the libraries have chosen to include multiple making methods for their patrons to explore. This fits with Abram's definition that makerspaces "provide access to a wide variety of tools and technology" (2013, 18).

To make the list a bit more complete, the responses that composed the *other* category on the survey are shown in the textbox. Additional technologies were added in 33 responses. They bring a bit more specificity to some of the survey options (e.g., Scratch or littleBits) and add interesting applications not included in table 4.1. For instance, having a presentation space with a stage is an intriguing addition to a library, as is an oscilloscope or a seismograph. Some other listed items likely should have made it onto the original survey from the start, such as papercrafts, the button maker, and video production equipment.

Again, even with the "others" added, the list surely does not reflect everything that is going on in library makerspaces, especially since it reflects the offerings of only 109 makerspaces. Taken together, the lists do provide you with approximately 84 options for your makerspace. The remainder of the book, particularly chapters 6 through 10, will identify other options as well. Recognizing a sampling of the universe of options for your makerspace to include can help you prepare to make choices.

⑥ Evaluating the Most Used Items in the Survey Makerspaces

Taking this process a bit further, you can look for guidance on what is actually being used in existing library makerspaces. In addition to the many examples from the literature that this book references, an additional question in the survey asked respondents to list the items or technologies that get the most use in their makerspaces. Fifty-six respondents answered the question, with all but a couple of them offering multiple technologies that are used the most. The most common responses were 3D printers (18 responses and 32 percent of respondents), video production and editing (9 responses, 16 percent), and sewing or sewing machines (4 responses, 7 percent). While respondents included many digital technologies in their selections, more classic options appeared, such as "paper, glue, and exacto knives." There were also interesting combinations of most-used items, such as "paracord bracelet materials and the books on app creation" or "marshmallow shooters and air rocket events, Arduinos." The patrons who use these makerspaces have varied interests and are perhaps not afraid to jump from more physical to more digital activities. The ethos of collaboration among makers of different forms can thrive in a coworking environment where multiple technologies and activities are supported.

◎ Assessing What Makerspaces Still Need

The final question in the survey asked respondents to discuss what they hoped to add to their makerspaces in the next year. Fifty-seven respondents with makerspaces already in place responded. The choices that recurred the most included a 3D printer (16 responses and 28 percent of respondents), more space or dedicated space (8 responses, 14 percent), a 3D scanner (7 responses, 12 percent), and adding workshops or having more public ways (e.g., maker faires) for makers to share what they have created (7 responses, 12 percent). For as many times as the 3D printer showed up in responses, there was a common thread of arts and crafts or handmade items in 14 of the responses (24 percent), with gardening, sergers (specialized sewing machines), and woodworking listed along with one respondent's hope for "more melding of technology and crafts e.g. soft circuitry."

◎ Choosing Making Options: Results from the Survey

In the same survey, respondents were asked how they decided which technologies they should offer in their makerspaces. They were guided to choose all options that applied to their makerspaces. The most popular response is "modeled on other makerspaces," chosen by 56 librarians (29 percent). This is certainly a popular technique for many physical and virtual changes in libraries, where tours, written accounts, and visits to websites can influence the development. Next came "input from educators" with 46 responses (24 percent), "suggestions from patrons" with 33 responses (17 percent), and "patron surveys" with 17 responses (9 percent). Looking to those who will use or guide the use of the makerspace seems like a logical method. The choice of "donations of equipment," with 15 responses (8 percent), reflects an interest from members of the community that goes further than mere words. As with any donation in a library, it may be a welcome addition or something unexpected and not immediately useful. There was also an *other* category with 27 responses (14 percent), most of which reiterate one of the earlier choices, along with 4 or 5 responses that added the element of staff suggestions or interests in helping decide on the makerspace's offerings.

◎ Making Decisions about Making in Your Library

The methods defined here can certainly guide any prospective makerspace creator in gathering input and information to shape one's space. The following section examines these methods in detail and suggests ways to use the inputs of data, options for making, and perhaps donated items to build a space that can positively affect a library's community. Remember that making takes many forms, and while technology may play a heavy role in some makerspaces, others use more handcrafted approaches with recycled materials (Roscorla 2013). The world of choices for making awaits!

Find Other Examples in Libraries

So how do you locate other library makerspaces? As with many finding tasks, a little Googling will get you started (e.g., "makerspaces libraries public"). What is quite helpful to this task is the fact that so many library makerspaces are out there. Although just a few have been chronicled at length in the library literature—for example, Fayetteville Free

Library (Britton and Considine, 2012), Westport Public Library, the HYPE Teen Center at the Detroit Public Library (Britton, 2012)—many others have been written up in local news sources and will likely appear in library publications over time. The bibliography can point you toward many profiles of library makerspaces. Also, the 17 library makerspaces that are profiled in this book provide you with examples to learn from and individuals to contact for more information. A growing web resource is MakerBridge (http://makerbridge.si.umich.edu), which provides a forum for library makerspaces to share their questions and their presence.

There is a danger inherent in finding model library makerspaces in that you will be moved to duplicate their offerings and services without further consideration. That could lead to an easy process of matching equipment purchases and copying program ideas, without enough attention paid to one's own community. The greater value in this research and the conversations that might occur is to see what is working for another library (ideally, several other libraries), to talk with the staff to see how they made their choices, and then to apply this process in your own environment. The examples of other libraries can provide assistance in comparing competing products, testing the efficacy of programming methods, and lending clues to developing the activity in another community. These experiences also let you envision making at work in another library setting.

Find Other Makerspaces in Your Community

Another route to take is to locate a makerspace in your community. This opportunity can provide you advice from those with expertise in making equipment and processes, as well as gaining insights on programming and perhaps gaining a partner or source of volunteers for your own making effort. Here are some methods for finding makerspaces:

- Makerspace.com has a directory of makerspaces at http://makerspace.com/makerspace-directory.
- The *Make:* magazine site has a list of maker community groups at http://makezine.com/maker-community-groups.
- The MakerMap (themakermap.com) is an open-source directory of making organizations and sites that provides a browsable and searchable Google Maps interface to help you locate local and regional makers.
- Similar sources include Hackerspaces (hackerspaces.org/wiki/List_of_Hackerspaces) and MIT's Fab Lab List (fab.cba.mit.edu/about/labs).

Local makers can give you insights into what types of making are already going on in your community or region. That might open up complementary making opportunities for you to hold in the library, or it could point out unmet interests or needs that you could take on. Visiting a makerspace could provide excellent how-to information for your library makerspace development, and joining one can give you hands-on experience with products and machines before you buy them yourself. The spirit that moves libraries to share making technologies can benefit you as you make plans and develop funding for your space.

Consider Staff Talents

As many library makers have discovered, their own colleagues can help guide the direction of a makerspace through the input of their talents and interests. You might have no idea that someone on your staff is a woodworker, or program Arduinos, or have a talent with crafts away from the job. They might be interested in teaching others how to do that activity, even if that might not be their regular role at the library. You might be inspired by the staff talents that you find, to pursue making options that match those talents and to even seek to alter staff roles to help bring a makerspace into fruition. Finding capable individuals to help patron makers and to help guide the development of a space can be a challenge, but do not forget to ask around as you begin thinking about a makerspace. It can lead to some interesting opportunities, even if it is someone taking on an occasional workshop or covering a few hours of time assisting patrons in an open makerspace environment. And if there are individuals on staff who know a bit more about 3D printing or soldering than you do, they can help you plot out the realities of working with that technology.

Be Inspired by Makers

While this can go hand in hand with visiting local makerspaces or talking with talented staff members, opportunities to watch or read about makers at work can provide ideas for making to add to your library. Recommended sources for this are located everywhere, from craft fairs to local businesses. You could have some interesting conversations with a maker that might lead to someone teaching a session at your library. Three books that provide a sampling of makers that might inspire you are one by Bob Parks (2006) that profiles 91 makers and their projects, another by Jennifer Causey (2013) that examines 30 makers in Brooklyn, and a final one by Karen Wilkinson and Mike Petrich (2014) that examines the works of 150 makers. The idea here is to seek out artists, chefs, manufacturers, electricians, and others—whether in person or on PBS—who might exhibit a type of making that you think your patrons could benefit from.

Consider Other Partners

Beyond local makers, there may be other organizations in your community that you could connect with and find a mutual making activity or partnership. The engineering club on your campus might have a 3D printer but lack the space to keep it running. There might be local crafters who would love the opportunity to gather in your library and would be happy to have more individuals join their group. Science teachers or a robotics team in the local schools might support and use the STEM-based educational opportunities that your school or public library makerspace provides. As you begin looking around your community, think about what might interest a potential partner in working with you in a making activity, and talk about your thoughts whenever the opportunity arises. There may be common ground available in places and with groups you never considered.

Gathering Input from Patrons and Other Interested Parties

As you shape your makerspace plans, you should consider not only the views and interests of established groups but also those of the individuals who you hope will use the makerspace. Surveys are a great method for marketing your eventual makerspace (it lets people know that you are adding something new) and for gauging your community's interest in specific making activities. You can easily create simple web surveys using Google Docs or SurveyMonkey, and you will find many examples of past surveys by Googling "makerspaces survey." You can also run off printed copies of the same survey to capture individuals whom you might not reach through electronic means. For a combined version of these two approaches, you could also have a web survey in your browser on a tablet that you encourage library visitors to fill out. Apart from individual surveys, you can use whiteboards or flip pads on easels to gather ideas from individuals who might not have time to fill out a full survey but who could respond quickly to a single question. The "Makerspace Playbook" includes sample surveys for potential makers and for those who might be interested in mentoring in your makerspace (Makerspace.com 2013).

Seek Donations

No makerspace would want to limit its program to what can be supplied by donors, but why not seek out interested people and groups in your community who might be willing to provide materials? It never hurts to ask and see what local groups or businesses might be able to offer. You want the needs of your makers to define how the space grows in services and activities, but donations from groups and individuals can be a part of that definition process. As you brainstorm donation possibilities, consider these questions:

- Could you work cooperatively with a local makerspace on a maker faire and then have it donate some teaching time at the library?
- Could you make the case that your projects contribute to STEM education and then have a company donate materials toward improving its future workforce?
- Are the projects that you are working on able to turn someone else's trash into your maker's treasures? Companies with scrap materials to dispose of might be willing to pass some of them your way.

Form a list of items that you can really use and would accept from donors. This will help you ensure that the donations reflect the activities that you have in mind and will not just sit around and take up space (Martinez and Stager 2013). This is not to say that the donation of a piece of equipment or supplies that you never expected is always a head-ache. It might open up a new set of workshops or projects and could connect you with another partner in the community who would use these items or teach your makers to use them. It is a good idea, though, to be realistic about what you can actually use the equipment for and how soon it could be put into use. If someone donates a jet engine for your makerspace, how does that fit into the skills and interests of your makers? Beyond local sources, look at TechSoup.org for technology donations for nonprofit organizations and libraries and Donors Choose (http://www.donorschoose.org) for donations to schools.

Getting the Right Mix for Your Community

The makerspace has to benefit its makers, and your goal in gathering input and choosing the right making activities is to form a space that fulfills this expectation. Keep in mind that the makerspace is not a "one and done" sort of enterprise. You will start off trying to interest people in the types of making that both you and they thought would be great to learn. Some of these types will pan out, and others may fall by the wayside after a time. The makerspace will need to expand its offerings to meet new needs and interests or to reach deeper into one area of knowledge to take makers toward greater expertise.

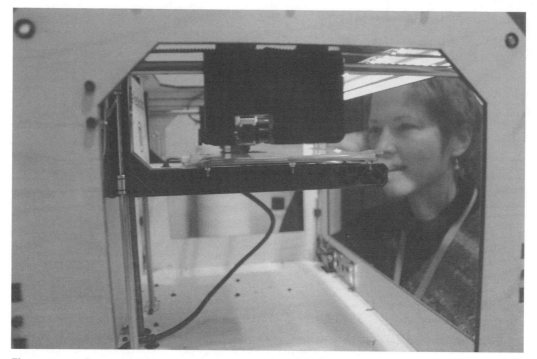

Figure 4.1. 3D printer in action at Anythink Brighton. *Provided by Aaron Bock*

You will have to stay aware of new developments in making, and chapter 12 offers a variety of means to do so. Heed Farkas's (2013) warning that not every new thing is "the" thing for your patrons. The initial surveys of your makers cannot be the end of your information gathering either. A regular assessment of patrons' reactions to workshops and open making times will guide your development. Some choices of technologies and activities will be clear-cut, but do not be afraid to take a chance on adding something interesting to your makerspace. The suggestions in this chapter will help you get ideas and start your makerspace moving. As Martinez and Stager advise, "don't let shopping get in the way of action" (2013, 89).

Library Makerspace Profile: Anythink Brighton, Brighton, CO

http://www.anythinklibraries.org/location/anythink-brighton

http://www.anythinklibraries.org/thestudio

Aaron Bock, Technology Guide

How Did Your Makerspace Come to Be?

Bock works at one branch library in a medium-sized library district. The space was funded through a Library Services and Technology Act grant. The libraries were able to start a digital learning lab at another branch through a different grant, and Bock's boss decided to go a different route. They applied for and received a Library Services and Technology Act grant to launch a makerspace. A team of four librarians and their manager discussed what they would like to do and which skills they had. One librarian was interested in arts and crafts (sewing, knitting, quilting, etc.). Another librarian was interested in photography. Bock was curious to add a 3D printer (figure 4.1) and learned some CAD (computer-aided design) applications and 3D design software to help with this. The team thought about what it was interested in and what might be interesting to add in the future to keep the space moving.

They have been open since December 2012. They have a low-tech feel in their space, with sewing and knitting types of maker work, but they also added a 3D printer, 123D Design, and digital photography. They had a meeting room that was not being used, and they decided to use it for their space. Everything is on wheels for easy movement.

Most of everything in the makerspace has been covered by the grant. They will need to come up with new grant funding to expand into new equipment. There is some funding from the library budget to keep the makerspace going and to keep buying consumable materials. Bock also teaches basic computer classes and has a budget from that which he can use for makerspace activities as well. They just need to keep finding funds to make larger additions to their offerings.

Who Uses It?

Anythink Brighton holds many programs throughout the year aimed at both teens and adults. It has held LEGO WeDo programs for kids. It has taught the basics of sewing with sewing machines and sergers to groups of all ages and skill levels. It is developing a formal artists-in-residence program that partners creative community members with library customers as mentors to help hone skills using the tools in "The Studio." The local school district is focused on STEM education and is pushing opportunities for learning outside the classroom. The makerspace fills a real need in the community.

How Do You Market the Makerspace?

The libraries' communications department branded its makerspace as "The Studio." It promotes The Studio through events at the library, programs, articles in local media, and presentations about the program at conferences across the country. It also provides tours to other librarians and community members so that they can see The Studio in action. The Studio at Anythink represents the library's approach to participatory, hands-on learning. Both the makerspace at Anythink Brighton and the digital learning lab at Anythink Wright Farms are under the umbrella of The Studio. They are working to expand this concept districtwide in the next 3 years. Since their equipment is mobile, they can transport it from branch to branch to support programs at the two branches. For instance, Bock holds some Arduino and MaKey MaKey workshops with equipment that he can easily travel with.

Who Supports It?

The librarians in the branch hold programs in The Studio and assist people. They also have artists in residence from the community come in and offer classes. For instance, they have provided portrait and digital photography classes. The library staff members have talked to various community organizations, including local art schools, and are trying to make plans to share equipment with them and find ways to share skills among the organizations.

What Does It Include?

The library offers Arduino and MaKey MaKey programming in-house. It is still looking at the possibility of checking out Arduino kits, but it first has to increase its staff members' comfort with them. It also has a 3D printer, CAD software, digital photography, textile arts, and computer guts.

How Do You Stay Aware of Developments in Makerspaces?

Bock follows random websites that turn up in Twitter and on Boing Boing, and he talks to people in the community about projects they are working on. His plan is to identify stuff that sounds cool and then get ideas of how to use it in the library. He also participates in local maker faires.

What Do You See Happening in Your Makerspace in the Next Year?

The present situation is people enjoying what is there and participating in workshops that give them the ability to find new skills and talents. Bock always asks people at workshops what else they would like the library to offer, and he takes those opportunities to recruit talent to teach workshops. The library has people interested in melding Arduinos and craft projects together. Right now, there is not much time that the space is open, due to limited staff availability. The library might need to move toward leaving it open more often to give people a chance to play with the equipment. For now, Bock will sit in the space and work on programming or curriculum for workshops and see if people stop in with questions.

What Is Your Advice to Others Who Would Like to Create a Makerspace?

Your makerspace does not have to be big. You can start small and find needs that your community has. The library found that everyone was excited about low-tech sewing and crafting, so staff went with it. You can start with basic activities and expand as you go, fostering larger investments of time and equipment. It is less scary to start that way.

⊚ Library Makerspace Profile: CreateSpace, Middletown Free Library, Lima, PA

http://www.middletownfreelibrary.org/#!createspace/c20ax

Mary Glendening, Library Director

How Did Your Makerspace Come to Be?

The library was awarded a Library Services and Technology Act grant. A library board member who had a personal interest in making supported the idea of pursuing the grant. Glendening had participated in some making activities ahead of this but really was not thinking of those activities as "making" per se. Lots of people are making things without realizing that they are part of the maker movement. It is bigger than just technology: cooking is making, for instance. The library was also selected to be an affiliate camp site for Maker Camp in the summer of 2013, and that generated excitement. It used that experience to gather making materials, try out forms of making, introduce the community to the idea of making, and build interest toward a January 2014 opening of the library makerspace.

The company of its now former board member with an interest in makerspaces has pledged to support the library for a couple of years with some funds. The library is an official open lab site for Curiosity Hacked (http://www.curiosityhacked.org), a national nonprofit aimed at teaching kids STEAM skills through making, and that group recommended that the library charge a small materials fee or other small fees to provide resources for some of the projects. It definitely wants to remain accessible to its public so that people can participate in the makerspace. The library will sell T-shirts or products made in the makerspace at an arts and crafts/maker faire event.

Who Will Use It?

The summer Maker Camp generated a loyal following of families for the forthcoming CreateSpace. Glendening is gathering ideas for the makerspace through a survey, and many parents have completed it. She expects that this will lead to many kids involved in the space. The focus of the Library Services and Technology Act grant was to provide makerspace technologies for small businesses in the library. Business owners are interested in the opportunity to create videos and podcasts.

How Do You Market the Makerspace?

The library has set up Facebook and Twitter accounts. It is using part of the grant funds to create brochures that describe its offerings. As part of a larger library system that reaches beyond its immediate community, it can market the makerspace to a larger population. Glendening has sent out press releases and is planning a launch event that will feature several maker activities set up in the room. It has a page on its library website dedicated to the space where it can advertise upcoming programs and new developments. It has also created some items with the 3D printer that it can use in the library to increase interest and in other publicity opportunities.

What Does It Include?

CreateSpace is not planned as a dedicated space in the library that will be set up at all times, although it is working toward having a dedicated spot eventually. The library is planning it as a pop-up makerspace that can be deployed and assembled as needed. There is now space to store items in the library. The maker items are all portable and can be taken to schools and elsewhere in the community. The items include 3D printers, a digital audio recording station (composed of a Mac mini and some consumer-friendly recording and editing applications), iPads, and a Surface Pro tablet with an attachment that will let it handle video recording and editing. The library has both a Makerbot Replicator 2 and a Replicator 2X, so as the library's maker population adds more skills, it can move on to more advanced equipment.

It has purchased some littleBits kits, and since it is sponsored by an audio recording studio, it has a lot of audio recording equipment. The kits are great for kids to handle and see how things interact between the physical and digital worlds. The library will be adding a vinyl cutter and sewing machines, but it is drawing the line at woodworking since it really does not have the room for it. The space is something of a combination of a makerspace and a digital and audio creation space. Some people who responded to the survey indicated interest in converting their VHS tapes to DVD, so Glendening is researching options to make this happen.

The grant funds will enable the library to pay some instructors to come in and teach workshops, but it will also have open lab times as well for people to experiment.

How Do You Stay Aware of Developments in Makerspaces?

Glendening attended MakerFaire in New York City, and that was an excellent experience. She follows several makers on Twitter, which has helped her keep up and make connections with people. She has found that just Googling for articles and experiences is very helpful, especially to see how other makerspaces are set up and functioning. The Curiosity Hacked site is great resource for instructional materials. By becoming a part of the organization, the CreateSpace will now have access to a larger trove of instructional materials and a support community through Google hangouts.

What Do You See Happening in Your Makerspace in the Next Year?

CreateSpace opened in January 2014. One of the first programs it offered is "Minecraft in Real Life," which involves using curriculum designed to teach circuits based on elements from Minecraft. Having an 8-year-old has given Glendening a lot of ideas and insights, as well as opportunities to talk with other parents and their kids. She says that the library's teen advisory group is starting up and beginning to generate ideas for more directions.

What Is Your Advice to Others Who Would Like to Create a Makerspace?

Figure out what your community wants and start small. Do not get hung up on 3D printers; there is so much else that you can do for less of an investment. Participating in Maker Camp, even if you are not an official site, is a great way to get started. There are lots of options to make great stuff even without fancy equipment. Figuring out why creations worked or did not work is a great activity that can really teach you how to teach the making to others. Give yourself time to tinker with stuff.

Ⓖ Key Points

For patrons to start using the library's makerspace, decisions need to be made about which making options to add. Some key points to recall from the chapter follow:

- Existing library makerspaces exhibit a myriad of maker technologies and activities.
- Use a variety of methods to seek out options for and guidance on making in a proposed makerspace.
- The makerspace must meet the needs and interests of its community.

The next chapter addresses the crucial question of funding to carry a makerspace forward.

References

Abram, Stephen. 2013. "Makerspaces in Libraries, Education, and Beyond." *Internet@Schools* 20 (2): 18.

Britton, Lauren. 2012. "The Making of Maker Spaces, Part 1: Space for Creation, Not Just Consumption." *Digital Shift* (blog). October 1. http://www.thedigitalshift.com/2012/10/public-services/the-makings-of-maker-spaces-part-1-space-for-creation-not-just-consumption/.

Britton, Lauren, and Sue Considine. 2012. "The Making of Maker Spaces, Part 3: A Fabulous Home for Cocreation." *Digital Shift* (blog). October 1. http://www.thedigitalshift.com/2012/10/public-services/the-makings-of-maker-spaces-part-3-a-fabulous-home-for-cocreation/.

Causey, Jennifer. 2013. *Brooklyn Makers: Food, Design, Craft, and Other Scenes from a Tactile Life.* New York: Princeton Architectural Press.

Farkas, Meredith. 2013. "In Practice. Spare Me the Hype Cycle." *American Libraries* 44 (5): 23.

Makerspace.com. 2013. "Makerspace Playbook." http://makerspace.com/wp-content/uploads/2013/02/MakerspacePlaybook-Feb2013.pdf.

Martinez, Sylvia Libow, and Gary Stager. 2013. *Invent to Learn: Making, Tinkering, and Engineering in the Classroom.* Torrance, CA: Constructing Modern Knowledge Press.

Parks, Bob. 2006. *Makers: All Kinds of People Making Amazing Things in Garages, Basements, and Backyards.* Sebastopol, CA: O'Reilly Media.

Roscorla, Tanya. 2013. "Why the 'Maker Movement' Is Popular in Schools." *Center for Digital Education* (blog). August 14. http://www.centerdigitaled.com/news/Maker-Movement-Popular-Schools.html.

Wilkinson, Karen, and Mike Petrich. 2014. *The Art of Tinkering.* San Francisco: Weldon Owen.

CHAPTER 5

Budgeting for a Makerspace

AS LIBRARIES CONSIDER ADDING A MAKERSPACE, the question of funding can open doors to bring a space into being, or it can serve as an unyielding barrier to moving ahead. A successful grant proposal ensures that a library can purchase materials for a makerspace because that is the very nature of a grant: it has to produce the activity that the proposal promised. However, setting artificial requirements for what the makerspace must have while having no access to the requisite funds can make a dream makerspace appear impossible to achieve. Making is not free, but it can be inexpensive. The previous chapter examines gathering ideas on what sorts of making should happen in the library. This chapter turns toward establishing a budget for the makerspace and finding funding to make a dream come true.

Pricing Your Makerspace

So what expenses go into forming and sustaining a library makerspace? Given the range of options and levels of service, a makerspace could conceivably be implemented for a few hundred dollars (e.g., a series of Arduino sets and workshops taught by library staff members; an investment in paper, scissors, and paint for a more artistic focus), or it could run into many thousands or even millions of dollars (e.g., adding multiple 3D printers, scanners, and computers; creating a new building full of laser cutters, computer numerical control machinery, and other prototyping equipment; "Cool Stuff" 2013). Cavalcanti (2013) offers a detailed list of categories and prices for both the costs of a private makerspace and the income outlook that it might have. It is definitely worth a look to make sure that you are not missing something. Identifying potential costs as you plan your makerspace can help you decide what is feasible to add to the library. The process can also help you build sets or groups of future additions that can be added in stages as funds become available. As you create a wish list of items and activities using the methods in chapter 4, you can then turn to your budget and assess what you can really afford. What follow are some cost categories to plan for as you develop your makerspace.

Staffing

Who will support your makerspace activities? Will your current library staff members take on the additional duties as needed, or will they shift some of their time away from lower-priority tasks? Will you identify dedicated staff members to staff the makerspace, or will you spread the responsibility for the space throughout the staff? Will you depend on volunteers whom you recruit specifically for the makerspace to cover the space's open hours or other programming? Or will you hire new staff to take on the makerspace duties or allow current staff to shift over to this work?

These questions point at issues involving both the nature of the makerspace and the expectations that you have for staff. There is a sliding scale of makerspace activity and availability that needs to be decided on before you can assess staffing, and the examples given in chapter 3 can help you make these decisions. Your makerspace may not be a set place in the library but rather mobile equipment that is used both inside the library and in various outreach locations in your community. You may have only monthly makerspace programs in place or a limited set of times when the space is available for open use by patrons. Once you figure out how often and in what form your makerspace will be available, you can address the amount of staffing that those activities will require.

Chapter 11 covers methods for offering makerspace services and ways to consider making use of staff and volunteer time. The key takeaway from this section is that personnel costs have the potential to be the highest ongoing input into your costs. Starting to sketch out your needs now is essential.

Equipment

For questions about equipment, chapter 4 is the place to further discuss how to identify options to include in the makerspace. Once you have a list of activities and equipment in hand, you should price out the bigger-ticket items, from computer numerical control routers to video-editing stations and from 3D scanners to green screens. You can then move along to more affordable items, estimating the numbers that you will need of each. A great strategy is the idea of starting with a wish list that can be assessed for costs and then winnowed down to essentials, as demonstrated in the profile of the Richland Library in chapter 3. While a wish list can be mindful of other budget considerations, such as limitations of space or staffing, it can also be used as a long-term, modifiable planning document. You might add and price technologies that you are not sure you are ready to accommodate, with the idea that if they are too expensive or too involved to implement right away, you can keep them in mind for later additions. The main thing here is not to forget to settle on some technologies and get their acquisition costs down on your budget.

Space Addition and Renovation

Perhaps a given library makerspace will not use space in the library, or it can fit into already existing spaces (e.g., a meeting or group study room, a newly opened-up corner of the reference area following the removal of shelving). If this is your library, you may be able to skip this section of the budget. But if your makerspace plan involves designating a separate space and putting up walls or making a substantial change to an existing space, even adding carpet, then you will have some costs to add to the budget. You might be so fortunate to be able to piggyback on another project for the library, school, or campus, in which your makerspace area can be added to a larger project to add an addition or build an entire new branch or other facility. This can help you collaborate in the larger change that is already planned and not have all the costs associated with your makerspace. More often, though, the makerspace is being developed within an existing structure, with some options for renovation or some additional walls. Aside from these more involved renovations, it is good to consider whether the area you are working in will need more electrical outlets or network drops to accommodate the equipment you are adding. Be sure to walk out the space and think of anything that would help the makerspace work really well there. As with the equipment wish list, you may identify changes for the next time around or once additional funding is available after the makerspace is well established in the library.

Furniture

Now that you have considered what the area of the makerspace will look like, who will be working there, and what stuff will go into it, it is essential to have something for people to make upon. It may be that you already have furniture to repurpose from other areas of the library or the area that you are converting into the makerspace: computer furniture, tables, chairs, and whatnot. But if you are adding new technologies and you lack pieces of furniture to set them on, this should go into your thinking. Rolling carts and other contrivances to hold equipment or materials for a more mobile makerspace experience could be included in this category. Chapter 6 through 10 note any specific furniture needs that the kinds of making profiled in those chapters might require. The key here is to make your makerspace comfortable and functional for people to create in it.

Consumables

Remember the paper! It is all well and good to budget for a top-of-the-line multifunction device for your printing and copying needs and overlook the multiple reams and sizes of paper that you will need to buy over the months and years to use it. Many making activities cannot be completed without consumable items, such as paint, plastic, wire, and even paper. Do not forget to work a cost estimate for these refillable materials in your budget. Chapters 6 through 10 have sections that remind you about consumable items that you will need to have on hand and regularly replace for your making activities. The

"Makerspace Playbook" (Makerspace.com 2013, 75, 77) also has two lists of consumable items that can be helpful for coming up with your own list.

Training

Very clear decisions will need to be made on who is responsible for learning, teaching, and guiding the making in your makerspace. No one may need to be the jack-of-all-trades with skills from origami to soldering to 3D design, but you need to determine who on your staff will have a central role in planning and running the space. It can be a single coordinating individual or a team approach. Making skills may already be present among your staff members, but even in the best-case scenarios, you will need to allow for time to hold training sessions and for staff members to try out equipment and other technologies to achieve a level of comfort. Beyond training library staff members, you will need to think about who will teach patrons to work with the makerspace materials. Again, you may have interested and skilled individuals on the staff, but you may also need to reach out to volunteers or paid instructors. The survey of library makerspaces found that they most often had library staff members teach classes (76 responses for 49 percent of all responses). Volunteers (42 responses, 27 percent) and paid instructors from beyond the library (20 responses, 13 percent) were the other two most common choices, with a few respondents mentioning information technology staff or student staff members as other possible sources to lead training sessions.

Outreach and Events

Some of your operating costs will also involve expenses associated with holding workshops, mobile events, or mini–maker faires. Aside from the already covered overhead items of space, staff, equipment, and furniture, you may have to increase the amount of consumables that you would need to accommodate workshop participants. You might also need to budget for additional marketing, transportation, and giveaway costs for these events. If you are committing to offering making in your library or through your library programs, you need to invest in the process.

Creating a Budget

As you juggle and weigh the categories of potential expenses for your makerspace, the time comes when you should start setting them down in a more fixed form. Be as realistic as possible in deciding on figures for the items in your budget. The research that you have completed on product choices and other libraries' implementations will help you fill in the budget lines. Additional resources for you to consult are included in chapter 12. At times, you will need to estimate amounts for situations where you cannot find an exact model for your planned service or where firm figures are unavailable. You may find it useful to plot out your items on a document like the library makerspace budget worksheet shown in table 5.1.

Sample budgets or equipment lists may also be useful guides and indicate additional expenses that you had not yet considered. The "Makerspace Playbook" (Makerspace.com 2013, 61) has a sample budget that shows some equipment and item costs; it also has a graduated cost perspective depending on how much money a library has available and what additional items can then be added. Jeri Hurd, whose Western Academy of Beijing

Table 5.1. Library Makerspace Budgeting Worksheet

CATEGORY	ITEM DESCRIPTION	NO. OF ITEMS	COST PER ITEM	TOTAL COST
Staffing				
Library staff time				
Paid instructors				
Equipment				
Must-haves				
Could-uses				
Maybe-somedays				
Furniture				
Consumables				
Training				
Staff training expenses				
Paid instructors				
Outreach and Events Costs				
Marketing				
Additional consumables				
Transportation				

makerspace is profiled in chapter 6, shared her equipment list at http://www.scribd.com/doc/179096661/makerspace-equipment-pdf. A makerspace budget for the Detroit Public Library Teen HYPE Center, created by Jeff Sturges, is available from a link under the "Budgets" category at the Mt. Elliott Makerspace site (http://www.mtelliottmakerspace.com/makeamakerspace/). Sturges also provides a blank template document as an Excel file at the same location. You should also read through the library makerspace profiles located throughout this book for additional stories of finances and budgeting for makerspaces in libraries.

Funding a Makerspace

So what options are available to provide funding for a library makerspace? The choices available will mirror many of the funding choices available to libraries for any new program or services. Some of the main differences exist in specific grants or donation opportunities, which are detailed here. The first place to look for confirmation of useful methods for makerspace funding is in the results from the library makerspace survey.

Results from the Survey

The 2013 survey of library makerspaces asked respondents to indicate one or more of their sources of funding to start their makerspaces (sources shown in figure 5.1). Of the respondents, 55 (50 percent) said that funding came from the library budget, while 44 (40 percent) reported that they received money from grants, 21 (19 percent) received donations to start their makerspaces, and 16 (15 percent) requested additional funding from their parent organizations (colleges and universities, school districts, city or county governments, etc.). Another 16 (15 percent) responded that they found funding from other sources, including variations on the grants category, friends of the library groups, capital and state building funds, and city and local investors. A total of 152 choices were spread out among the 109 respondents, indicating that each library makerspace averaged approximately 1.33 funding sources.

Making Your Case

So how do you convince others that you need a makerspace? Before jumping into the available sources for funding, a common requirement for seeking any type of funding is the ability to articulate what you need the funds for and why this might be a good idea. Earlier chapters in the book discuss reasons to form a makerspace and can certainly be returned to for arguments to buttress your own reasoning. You need to be able to summarize what you hope the space will accomplish for the potential makers who will use it. As well, you should tie the goals for the makerspace in with the mission of the library and the larger educational goals of your organization. Martinez and Stager (2013, 187–98) offer a chapter in their book that works through various means for making the case for a makerspace in a school, including rebutting questions or statements that individuals might raise against a proposal. Many of the approaches are adaptable to other library settings.

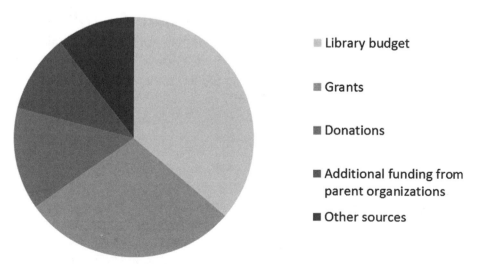

Figure 5.1. Sources of makerspace funding from the survey of library makerspaces.

TEXTBOX 5.1.

WHY LIBRARIES ADDED A MAKERSPACE

"Libraries are increasingly about a third area of service provision. Not only do we continue to do the important work of preservation and access as we have done all along, but increasingly there is an expectation that libraries will support content creation."

"A MakerSpace provides members with new skills, a place to share with others and a place to create something with their hands, imagination and tools!"

"Hands-on learning is an important part of learning in general, where students can start to develop skills for self-directed learning about topics that they are passionate about."

"We want to provide an on-ramp to the larger Maker Movement, as well providing the community access to technology beyond items normally purchased for home use."

"The library needs to support all literacies and encourage students to become content creators, rather than content consumers."

"For people in our community to work together, to discover, to share."

"We are providing teens the opportunity to learn real life skills that they otherwise might not have access to."

The library makerspace survey included a question for respondents to express how they explain to others why they added a makerspace. Examples from their statements are shown in the textbox.

These statements and the Wordle of terms taken from the responses to that question in figure 5.2 can help you build your own explanation of your space. That explanation can then be modified to create grant proposal statements or elevator speech–length expressions, depending on your audience and purpose.

Finding Space in the Library Budget

Every library is different, and every library budget is different. That being said, every library can find some money to start up a makerspace, given that the entry point for a makerspace can be fairly low. Money for new initiatives is rarely just lying around, and it tends to come at a subtle shifting of priorities from one area of service toward another and perhaps in a competitive process among various new ideas that the library staff are considering. Libraries may be able to set aside funding from one year to carry into the next and use the combined funds to start a makerspace. There may be end-of-fiscal-year money available that must be spent quickly, and makerspace proponents should have their justification ready to offer up when the time is right. Not every budget or spending process will allow or encourage these activities, and not every budget will have flexibilities

Figure 5.2. Words used by survey respondents to describe their reasons for having a makerspace.

in budget lines that allow a reduction in book spending or database subscriptions to be used for starting a makerspace.

Library staff and administrators need to ask themselves whether they find the creation of a makerspace a priority for their institution: if not, then funding will have to wait for a change in priorities or for external funding to spark internal interest; if so, then they will seek where fluidities exist within the library budget that might free up a few hundred dollars here or a thousand dollars there that could be used to try out a makerspace. Perhaps a small investment in some Arduinos for a workshop or the hosting of a class or two provided by members of a local makerspace could serve as a meaningful trial balloon for future developments. Staff interest cannot be the sole driving force for the makerspace nor its sole funding source. But if the case can be made well to library administration, a small amount of money can usually be found.

Additional Organizational Funding

In some environments, there may be the opportunity for the library to seek additional onetime funds from its parent organization, which might be a college or university, a city, or a school district. It is definitely worth exploring if such funding is an option in your setting. This may be a defined process in that organization, or it may be completely new ground. A carefully explained proposal for funding that has a clear benefit to that larger organization could help you locate funds that will simply be impossible from other sources.

Finding Grants

There are a number of grant programs in place that could be pursued as possibilities for funding makerspaces. These include federal and state government programs, as well as grants from within library organizations, parent organizations such as schools and institutions of higher education, and local and national foundations. Talk with your local development staff or your state library for suggestions on possible funding sources. Some options to consider include an ongoing program of grants for "Learning Labs for Libraries and Museums" from the Institute of Museum and Library Services and the MacArthur Foundation (http://www.imls.gov/about/learning_labs.aspx). Federal grants funded by the Library Services and Technology Act and administered by state libraries may also provide opportunities for makerspace programs (see links to individual states at the American Library Association, http://connect.ala.org/node/138571). Some state libraries have offered specific funding programs to begin making, including New Jersey (http://librarylinknj.org/projects/makerspaces) and Idaho (http://libraries.idaho.gov/blogs/ericacompton/make-it-library-year-2-application-open).

Fund-Raising and Seeking Donations

Donations of equipment, materials, and time are addressed in chapter 4, but there is also the potential for funds to be donated to your makerspace effort. Crowdfunding opportunities are widely used for funding a variety of maker-led product launches and could also work for libraries interested in starting a makerspace. In the crowdfunding model, people interested in seeing a product produced commit money to the creator. Once the creator has met the funding goal, he or she can then produce the item and supply it to those who committed the money (Anderson 2012, 168). The maker is effectively given a boost in terms of marketing so that he or she can then keep making the product and selling it to others. Services such as Kickstarter (http://www.kickstarter.com) and Indiegogo (http://www.indiegogo.com) exist to manage the funding process, accepting funds from those who are interested in the project and ensuring that the goals are met. Libraries could set goals for the equipment needed to start a makerspace and could offer making opportunities to those who fund that equipment. Britton (2012) describes the Fayetteville Free Library using this technique to raise some of the funds it needed for its makerspace.

Charging Fees

As a whole, libraries are committed to providing access to expensive items of all kinds without expecting any payment from their patrons or perhaps just negligible amounts. They are not money-making ventures and are not generally focused on cost recovery. It is common for makerspaces run by companies or membership organizations to charge monthly or hourly fees for using equipment and to charge for supplies. Libraries running makerspaces need to at least consider a charging structure to make the budgets for their spaces work out.

In the survey of library makerspaces, 34 respondents indicated that they do charge patrons for using the makerspace. That group makes up 31 percent of the total number of respondents who completed the survey. The most common method for charging patrons is to charge for consumables used in the making, with 22 respondents (65 percent of those who charge) reporting such a charge. An additional respondent who does not charge patrons noted that patrons bring all their own supplies. Seven of those who responded (21 percent) charge a fee for classes or workshops. Three respondents (9 percent) charge a membership fee: two charge it to all patrons, while the other charges only nonresidents a fee for using the library's makerspace. Two respondents (6 percent) charge patrons an equipment use fee.

Putting It All Together

Budgeting for and funding a makerspace is not necessarily a quick and easy process. By carefully considering the needed elements for the space, you can create a clear budget to begin an initial operation. Combining several funding sources can then make what looks good on paper truly come to life. Above all, be prepared at all times with the story of why you would like to add a makerspace. Tell it often, and as your makerspace grows into reality, add successful instances to the tale. This will help you continue to find the funding you need.

⑥ Library Makerspace Profile: Allen County Public Library, Fort Wayne, IN

http://tekventure.org/maker-station/

Norman Compton, Manager of Access Fort Wayne

How Did Your Makerspace Come to Be?

The Allen County Public Library partnered with a local makerspace called TekVenture to bring maker activities and equipment to its main library. TekVenture operates out of a mobile classroom in a parking lot at the library. The library provides electricity, power, and data to the mobile classroom to support its operations. TekVenture has long been a membership organization and now offers a meetup space in its mobile unit at the library as well. It has provided two maker faires in downtown Fort Wayne; the one in the fall of 2013 was attended by 3,000 people. It hopes to hold this as an annual event.

The plan was then to bring some technology into the main library so that it could be used whenever the library is open. TekVenture has limited hours, holding open hours on a few evenings a week and 6 hours on Saturdays. The library staff added a 3D printer in the library's computer center 1 year ago, and since that time, they have built up a total of four 3D printers. They are pursuing STEAM-focused activities with Arduinos in the library. The goal now is to transition the computer center into a makerspace. They will move out the computers and leave more space for workshops. The TekVenture mobile classroom remains in place.

TekVenture's mobile classroom is packed with technology. It has a center aisle, with various technologies packed on either side. It has wood lathes, 3D printers, an Eggbot that decorates eggs, and other items. Staff are looking to add more industrial technologies, such as plasma cutters or metal lathes, but they cannot do this in the mobile facility. The library has a warehouse that it lets TekVenture check out as a possible expansion spot, but it was judged not quite the right location.

Funding for libraries is always limited, but the library's director felt strongly about supporting the service, and he found the funds to make it happen. Over a year ago, a young adult librarian was applying for a grant for a teen digital laboratory, but the proposal was unsuccessful. Since all the plans were made, the director asked how much would it cost. He then managed to find $14,000 for equipment, including Macs, a scanner, flip cams, and more, with the strongest part of the lab being the audio-recording capabilities. The audio studio has been so popular that a similar studio just opened that adults can use. This helps the library transition teens who use the space into another library area when they age out.

Who Uses It?

Most users of the 3D printing are in their 20s or younger; some are some engineers from local companies that make use of the equipment as well. The library has a Makerbot Replicator 2 at the staff desk that is open for the public to use. Anyone can come in with a design on a flash drive, put on the attached PC, and create a 3D item. Many designs are from Thingiverse.com and other online collections and are then tweaked by the patrons. It often takes a couple of tries to get a design working with the 3D printer and to have it print correctly. It definitely requires patience. One guy was trying to print a bicycle chain guard and had to rework the design to get it to print right since it was too large. Another guy was able to print a plastic clip to hook his gaming console to his smartphone. It would have cost him $20 to buy one. The library charges patrons $3 per item as a flat rate and only for items that print correctly. It keeps the printing accessible to anyone, finding it easier to charge out for the staff rather than having to calculate amounts of plastic used.

How Do You Market the Makerspace?

Since the library has a broadcast television station and does programming for additional public access cable channels, it created public service announcements to run on the channels. It also has a video wall in the main library that it can run the announcements on, plus YouTube, Facebook, and other social media to post things. The television station has been part of the library for 30 years, which means that staff members have extensive video experience. This really helps them support cameras, webcams, and other video creation activities in the makerspace. They always have cameras on hand when people make things so that they can capture the event for the makers to show off their creations.

Being aware of the community needs around them has helped tremendously. They are fortunate to be able to network with many nonprofit organizations through their community access channel connections. Science Central is a local science museum that they have worked with. The local Air National Guard base has a Star Base facility giving STEAM exposure to elementary students. The library is talking about doing some programming with it, bringing Star Base classes back to the library to use the makerspace. It has been talking with Ft. Wayne community schools, working with their career campus, and coming up with ideas for programming. It hopes to do more community programs in 2014. These programs will create a lot of buzz in the community and will bring people into the library. It has looked to the Chicago Public Library to see how it links its community programs and builds up library use. The library is a known, safe organization in the community, and that will really help it attract people to bring their kids to library programs.

What Else Do You See Happening in Your Makerspace in the Next Year?

People are coming to the main library for workshops and making products. Now the library staff are taking making experience out to their other 13 branches. There are meeting rooms in every branch that can be used for making-related programs, and the main library lends out 3D printers for each branch to use and train staff. A couple of the branches are already planning to renovate space to create permanent Makerspace rooms, with the Georgetown branch opening its makerspace in March 2014.

The young adult digital studio now has its own 3D printer, so it can add that to its offerings. The library has just completed an application to add a low-power FM radio station. This is an outgrowth of the television side of the library, but it will give opportunities for people to record programs in the makerspace and then broadcast their creations. The library will develop the radio station with new automation and software to make this possible. It is also expanding its government access and public access programming on cable television, with a goal of increasing the diversity of its programming and developing minority voices in the community.

What Is Your Advice to Others Who Would Like to Create a Makerspace?

You have to network. Get out and build face-to-face relationships inside and outside your community. It is helpful to have someone in the library who is passionate for the cause and wants to try things out and experiment with stuff. The library is trailblazing this service and trying to find out more options and opportunities from colleagues elsewhere. Also, you need to stay open to experiments. The library is piloting a self-serve conversion center where people can make electronic conversions from 3.5-in. discs to flash drives and VHS to DVD.

⊚ Library Makerspace Profile: Michigan Makers, Ann Arbor, MI

http://michiganmakersypsi.weebly.com

Kristin Fontichiaro, Clinical Assistant Professor of Information, School of Information, University of Michigan

How Did Your Makerspace Come to Be?

In Ann Arbor, there are many makerspaces, hackerspaces, and collaborative workspaces in place, including a commercial-grade makerspace and a long tradition of artists and craftspeople. When the Raspberry Pi appeared, the idea of a computer that was as cheap as a library book really captured the attention of Fontichiaro and her colleagues. She wondered what it would mean to introduce students to tools like this, and she talked with an alumna of the School of Information who worked in a local middle school. The former student organized a programming club at her school in which students were using Scratch and Python. She thought that her students would be interested in Raspberry Pi. As Fontichiaro brainstormed with a working group of faculty members and graduate students who gathered to start a maker effort, they thought about students' interests in more tactile experiences. For instance, they could start with paper engineering, origami, gift wrapping, and needlework and progress into squishy circuits, Scratch and Python, and then Raspberry Pi Arduinos.

Their discussions came to fruition as they formed Michigan Makers and started maker activities at the school in 2012. As the number of graduate student volunteers grew, they brought with them additional talents. The school in which they worked had sewing machines, and one of their volunteers loved to sew and agreed to teach students to sew. The kids at the school also offered to teach from their own interests and talents. One student taught his classmates how to use Minecraft mods. Another was interested in the Science Olympiad and led some sessions on Science Olympiad challenges. Michigan Makers began using the approach of using "windows" and "mirrors": windows are activities that students might not be familiar with, which they could be introduced to and try out; mirrors are activities or talents that students in the group already came with. For instance, last year's group had a lot of programming experience.

For the 2013–2014 school year, Michigan Makers moved to two schools. Both are low socioeconomic status, one of which provides free lunches to 100 percent of its students. They go to each school once per week, an hour ahead of when the school day ends. The mentors meet and figure out what to do for that week and what items or activities may be fading. They play around with their new ideas first and then mentor students by showing off what the mentors created. Finally, they unpack their supplies to be ready for the kids to appear.

Fontichiaro and her colleagues are meeting kids where they are and when they are ready. They want to start out with activities that students can do without adult intervention. One of the maker mentors who loves to crochet taught the kids to crochet. They have also had kids take appliances apart to see how they fit together. They now have a 3D printer that they are rolling out. They also provide some programming activities and some needlework. They tend to have seven to eight choices for students to work with. This requires the mentors to bring in a lot of materials, but they have found that the more choices the kids have, the better.

When the students plateau on something, the mentors remove it from their offerings. When they did this with crocheting, the students rebelled. The students tend to want less stimulating activities at the start of the year or at times that are stressful. There are also students who cannot sustain interest in more involved tasks at first but who build up to larger challenges over time.

The Michigan Makers have one of their pop-up makerspaces in an elementary school. The students there will build anything. The boys in the group really liked friendship bracelets, something that the mentors did not imagine that they would like. Students seek out relaxing things, and the mentors want them to feel welcome and get involved in making. They always keep origami paper and other stuff to putter with on hand. They back off and let kids putter but are also ready to jump in and help. At the elementary school, they have a whiteboard with a message on it covering what they are going to do that day. They meet with the students and provide a snack. The students like to show off what they created and typically show their projects off to the whole group. The maker time lasts about 90 minutes. Then the mentors debrief to see if the activities are working well and to decide what to shop for.

The other school that the Michigan Makers visit is a middle school. They tend to not have much of a meeting with the middle school students. The mentors just put a list of possible activities up on the board. Students branch off and work on their own or in small groups. After an hour of work, they have the students reflect on their experience in a journal. The students do not like to have a formal showing off of their projects. The mentors are just about to roll out a "Project Runway" project in which the middle school students will transform a long-sleeve T-shirt into a more fashionable creation.

One of the Michigan Makers' partners is Maker Works (http://www.maker-works.com), a local makerspace. Fontichiaro says that their definition of a makerspace is tools plus support plus community. The mentors provide more to the schoolchildren than just holding classes. The students want to be there. For these kids, being around adults that are there for them is great. The mentors see the model of hackerspaces at work in the schools: places to hang out as well as work on things. Fontichiaro reflects that public libraries have addressed making by sending people away with books on activities. She recalls that the Memphis Public Library used to circulate garden tools, providing a step further than just lending a book on gardening.

How Have You Funded Your Efforts?

For the first year, the original middle school funded its projects. Michigan Makers then successfully wrote a grant proposal to the Michigan Association for Computer Users in Learning that enabled them to buy some Arduinos and guides for using them (they used free programming tools). Other items were self-funded by Fontichiaro from her faculty research funds. They received a grant from the University of Michigan Third Century Initiative and then a matching grant from the School of Information to study the impact of service-learning activities.

In addition to money, the Michigan Makers have received donations of items from students at the School of Information, including three computers, thread, and other items. Fontichiaro has learned that many individuals in her community hoard making supplies, hoping to eventually have time to work on projects. This has made it easy to find people who are willing to part with their supplies if she approaches them with a need. Another resource in Ann Arbor that has been very useful is the Scrap Box (http://www.scrapbox.com), a source for leftover materials donated by manufacturers that can be purchased inexpensively by the bag.

How Many Mentors Do You Have in the Program at One Time?

They began with 4 mentors and increased to 10 by the summer of 2013. For the 2013–2014 school year, the Michigan Makers had 10 mentors at one site and 4 at the other. It has been a wonderful experience for the participating graduate students, all of whom have found jobs due in part to their time as mentors. The graduate students are learning how well projects work for the kids and are gaining much practical knowledge about children's learning styles. The students have also been very helpful in suggesting ideas for activities, such as a littleBits and Korg synthesizer kit for the kids to build and make music with. Mentors generally participate in either the group at the elementary school or the one at the middle school. They also have a teacher from the elementary school and her middle school son who help out at the elementary school program.

A wonderful opportunity arose for the mentors and some of their makerspace partners with the creation of a series of books on making. Graduate students, librarians, and representatives of local makerspaces have written eight books in a series from Cherry Lake Publishing called "Makers as Innovators" (https://cherrylakepublishing.com/shop/show/10829). The Michigan Makers hope to add four more books to the series. They have found it extremely helpful to bring their manuscripts and page proofs into the schools before they go to press for students to test out.

What Do You See Happening in Your Makerspace in the Next Year?

At the middle school, a student is interested in pinhole cameras, and so the Michigan Makers will be exploring cameras in various ways (they have talked about Flickr Creative Commons and practiced digital photo editing so far). They are also working on the littleBits and Korg synthesizer there. They hope to expand their sewing activities. Fontichiaro likes the idea of holding appliance autopsies, since kids love to see what makes things work on the inside. They are trying to figure out how kids can do 3D modeling on their own, now that they have the 3D printer. They are just starting with e-textiles and conductive thread. They also hope to bring in some robotics and more LEGOs. A teacher recently donated a LEGO Mindstorms kit that should help with that. They also hope to bring Arduinos in and continue with their Scratch programming, perhaps adding some HTML. While the Michigan Makers are not planning to separate into boy and girl tasks at the schools, they are adding a Cameo laser cutter that can make stickers for notebooks as a way to welcome girls to the group.

What Is Your Advice to Others Who Would Like to Create a Makerspace?

Say yes to people's ideas! Try going with less money and getting a lot more done: buy a bunch of Arduinos, a sewing machine, or some screen printing kits. 3D printers are really cool but hard to work with for a large group of people. Not every academic library needs a 3D printer. Start small, and see where your community's interests are. Making is not just hacking or coding; makerspace is ideally about all kinds of making. Partnering is important: coworking can lead to intertwined technology projects and bring together multiple talents. Starting with screen-based activities may not build community well since the people need to look at one another to connect.

Key Points

Makerspaces are about tools, creativity, and community, but they also require money to get started and continue. Here are some key points from the chapter:

- Budgeting for a library makerspace is a key part of the planning process.
- Makerspaces can come together with a combination of internal and external funding along with donations of equipment and materials.
- Library makerspaces face the choice of charging or not charging fees and the subsequent question of which activities will have a charge.

Now the process of creating the makerspace will yield to five chapters that discuss particular types of making, starting with resources for audio, image, and video creation.

References

Anderson, Chris. 2012. *Makers: The New Industrial Revolution*. London: Random House Business Books.

Britton, Lauren. 2012. "A Fabulous Laboratory." *Public Libraries* 52 (4): 30–33.

Cavalcanti, Gui. 2013. "Making Makerspaces: Creating a Business Model." *Make:* (blog). June 4. http://makezine.com/2013/06/04/making-makerspaces-creating-a-business-model/.

"Cool Stuff to Outfit Your Makerspace." 2013. *American Libraries* 44 (1/2): 48–49.

Makerspace.com. 2013. "Makerspace Playbook." http://makerspace.com/wp-content/uploads/2013/02/MakerspacePlaybook-Feb2013.pdf.

Martinez, Sylvia Libow, and Gary Stager. 2013. *Invent to Learn: Making, Tinkering, and Engineering in the Classroom*. Torrance, CA: Constructing Modern Knowledge Press.

CHAPTER 6

Resources for Audio, Image, and Video Creation

IN THIS CHAPTER

▷ What Your Patrons Could Be Making

▷ Tools for Audio, Image, and Video Creation

▷ Refills Needed

▷ Special Space Requirements and Options

▷ Library Makerspace Profile: Penfield Library, State University of New York at Oswego, Oswego, NY

▷ Library Makerspace Profile: Western Academy of Beijing, Beijing, China

SO FAR, THIS BOOK HAS BEEN FOCUSED on the larger picture of the maker movement and where that movement can intersect with libraries. Now comes the point to start talking about specific making activities and how libraries can prepare to support them. To begin, the creation of audio and video is the focus. Capturing sounds and images as separate elements or combining them with video is an exciting task for a creator and one that libraries can support at multiple levels. Makers of any age and skill level can participate in some area of this realm of creation. Videos, sounds, and images permeate our experiences online and off, and these tools help turn media consumers into media creators (Jenkins, Ford, and Green 2013). This is a great way to get people started making things, partly because the tools involved have become easier to use and they are ubiquitous. To wit, in the informal survey of library makerspaces conducted for this book, this category of making accounted for 23 percent of the activities chosen by the 109 respondents. Explore the possible projects or needs that your community might have, and then consider equipment, software, and other tools that will make it happen in your library.

What Your Patrons Could Be Making

The first step in examining this category of making is to consider a variety of projects or examples that an individual could complete. This provides a goal to imagine. If a patron in your library wanted to take on one of these types of audio, image, or video making, what would he or she need? By no means can this list of projects be all-inclusive given the ever-imaginative minds of people. The hope is to suggest some possibilities for making in this area that are feasible and have succeeded elsewhere. See what intrigues you from the list that follows.

Digital Photography and Editing

Maybe your patrons want to try their hands at taking pictures and then learn how to adjust the resulting images into something more aesthetically pleasing or even more creative. Perhaps they want to learn to crop images and adjust the contrast or brightness of images. The library can provide support and instruction on using digital cameras, adjusting settings, using additional light sources, gaining a photographer's eye to frame the perfect shot, and editing images to get the best final image. There are many directions to take this work, and the nice thing for both the library and the patron is that there are multiple levels of complexity to pursue. People can start with the basics and progress through classes or advice from the makerspace staff. The makerspace can then be built up with more advanced tools as the makers come to need them.

Sample projects with image creation could include having patrons take pictures against a green screen and then showing them how to electronically substitute various backgrounds in the image (see figure 6.1). An example of doing this is in the library makerspace profile of the Poudre River Public Library in chapter 10, where this was part of a Day of the Dead–themed program. You could have patrons bring in an image as an electronic file or a printed image to scan and then have them use image-editing software to clarify or modify the image in some way. The library could also provide important educational guidance to patrons by teaching them about copyright and images, as the Penfield Library at SUNY Oswego (profiled later in this chapter) did through presentations on using Creative Commons images. Another useful skill would be to help patrons resize and post images to social media sites or for use on their own websites. There could be assignments or practice class projects in school or academic libraries where students take images related to what they are studying and share them with the class through presentation software or in the institution's learning management system. Anythink Brighton's staff (profiled in chapter 4) held portrait and digital photography classes for its patrons to improve their picture-taking skills.

Audio Recording and Editing

Audio recording gives patrons the ability to create a record of their words and voices, to share their thoughts with others, and perhaps to have a big break with their musical talents. Participants in an audio recording–equipped makerspace can learn about the

Figure 6.1. What you see vs. what we see. *Image provided through a CC BY 2.0 License by Category5 TV, http://www.flickr.com/photos/category5tv/6508366751*

various options that they have for recording audio and how to increase the quality of the recordings that they are making. A lot of ground can be covered from working with various types of microphones, choosing how to share and archive audio files, and even getting patrons to use their voices effectively to convey information and emotions. On the editing side, makers can learn how to edit out pauses and "umms," change the order of recorded segments, and mix audio files together. See figure 6.2 for an example of what this might look like.

Potential audio projects include patrons recording their thoughts for the purpose of sharing them with others as a podcast. Patrons could also interview family members or record their own memories to share as oral history. They could even combine audio recording with still images and create screencasts, which are useful for providing step-by-step instructions and demonstrations of activities, as well as an easy way to narrate a set of pictures or presentation slides. The Middletown Free Library (profiled in chapter 4) has a digital audio-recording station that local business owners are interested to use for creating videos and podcasts. Patrons in a wide range of ages might be interested in having a location to record music. At the Allen County Public Library (profiled in chapter 5), the teen audio studio was so popular that the library has opened a second one for adults to use. The Denver Public Library (profiled in chapter 8) has had a similar response from adults to its teen music studio. Of course, the noise-canceling qualities of your space can influence the types of activities that you support. Before you decide to create a sound studio, you need to think carefully about whether you want to have someone play the drums in your library and how you will reduce the sound.

Figure 6.2. Group audio recording room. *Image provided through a CC BY 2.0 License by Teaching and Learning with Technology (psutlt), http://www.flickr.com/photos/psutlt/6803213187/*

Video Recording and Editing

Video-related making can happen through equipment that the library allows patrons to check out, but it can also happen in a makerspace within the library building. There are many techniques that patrons can discover with fun and practical uses. As with other kinds of making, a skill can be introduced with a recreational project but then called on for other purposes. A green screen can be set up in the library to provide alternative backgrounds to filmed scenes or to create the effects of flying or driving behind those persons being filmed. Stop-motion animation of real-world objects can be recorded with a table and a backdrop. Animated images can also be created in software and used in a video. Once your users have captured video content, you can provide them the means to edit their video on standard public computers in the library or on specialized computers with greater speed and capacity for manipulating large video files. Recorded video can be cropped and reorganized and have effects added to it, along with music and audio files. See figure 6.3 for an example of a video-recording space.

Possible projects involving video include capturing all manner of activities with a camera and then using editing techniques to shape what has been captured. There are a many different directions to go, given the number of mobile devices and cameras that can capture video and the options for editing with software on desktops, laptops, and mobile devices. Patrons can make stop-motion videos by assembling scenes out of paper or drawing them on a white board—like this example from Make It @ Your Library, http://makeitatyourlibrary.org/technology/make-your-own-stop-motion-movie#.Uum2ed-K1GSo. They can create their own music videos, adding effects after filming through the use of a green screen or other video-editing software. Students can be filmed reading poetry, creating memorable ways to review coursework, creating public service announcements based on course research, and practicing conversations in a new language they are

Figure 6.3. VentureBeat video studio. *Image provided through a CC BY 2.0 License by Dylan Tweney (dtweney), http://www.flickr.com/photos/dylan20/6120889483*

learning. Patrons could be shown how to film and edit video and then how to post it on YouTube or Facebook to share it with a wider audience. Video projects give patrons a way to communicate their ideas and their creativity while learning technology skills.

One video-related project to add on here is the conversion of older video formats into newer ones. Patrons may have home movies on VHS videocassettes that they need to move to a more modern format so that the movies can still be viewed. With the demise of VCRs behind us and perhaps the end of DVDs not so far off, the next-best format may just be converting to a video file on a flash drive. The Allen County Public Library (profiled in chapter 5) is piloting a self-serve conversion center where patrons can move content from 3.5-in. discs to flash drives and VHS to DVD. There are certainly copyright and licensing considerations to consider here (i.e., you cannot make a DVD copy of a VHS version of title that others hold the copyright on), but it is a service that can aid your community.

Tools for Audio, Image, and Video Creation

There is such a sliding scale of equipment and software that you can work with such that it is easy to enter into these operations at ground level and then build upward to higher-quality results with more advanced products. It is true that many of these media-making possibilities can be done (at least simply) with a smartphone, a tablet, or a home computer, but there are other items that may be out of reach for your community. This is especially true of equipment or software that a patron might need for just a short time or occasional use (Quinn 2013). Another element to consider is that many of the tools that you might gather for these activities have other uses in more traditional library operations. They may already be on hand in the library—from computers and basic image and sound editors to iPads, microphones, and other items. You could also buy microphones and webcams for the makerspace, for instance, and then have your patrons or staff use them for Skype or Google Hangouts or other web-conferencing options. While some tools might be specialized, the majority will have multiple functions or purposes.

There are some key categories of equipment that library staff will need in order to offer image, audio, and video creation in their makerspace. Those categories are listed in the textbox and then examined at greater length here. A final way to illustrate technology needs in this area will be to work with the metaphor of the sliding scale and describe basic, enhanced, and advanced combinations of tools that can be offered.

Computers or Mobile Devices

Computers, tablets, or other mobile devices such as smartphones can be used for multiple facets of the image capture and editing process. Desktop and laptop computers (Windows, Macs, Linux, and Chromebooks) can handle the software that is needed to record and edit, and they can be used to plug in additional microphones, webcams, and other devices for recording purposes or to download saved images or video. Tablets (iPads, Android, and Surface) and smartphones generally have microphones and cameras built in and, being mobile, can go wherever the need to record takes you. They can also have apps installed on them to edit audio and video files.

A major consideration for media production with computers and similar devices is processing power and memory. Image, audio, and video files are generally rather large and require enough space to store them in a computer's hard drive or flash memory. This memory need can be alleviated to some degree by using cloud-based storage that puts the files on remote servers rather than keeping them on the local device. But another type of memory demand comes into play when you want to edit or otherwise modify the files. Sufficient RAM (random-access memory) needs to be available in the device to run editing software and process changes to the files.

Cameras

There are many types of cameras that can be utilized. Already mentioned are smartphones, tablets, or other devices (e.g., iPod Touch) that have built-in cameras and can easily share the images or video they record. Inexpensive point-and-shoot cameras can be used for still images or video recordings, which are then downloaded to a computer for editing or sharing. Additional lenses and peripherals such as flashes can be added to digital SLR (single-lens reflex) cameras to get higher-quality still images and video. Digital camcorders at various price points offer the potential for higher-quality video than what mobile devices can produce. Traditionalists may even opt for the ever-rarer experience of film cameras, especially if part of the makerspace draw is a darkroom.

Factors to consider when choosing cameras are very much tied to the type of projects that you expect to take on. Camera resolutions are improving across the board, with iPads and iPhones giving higher-definition images than cheaper point-and-shoot cameras or smartphones. If you are after ease of use and not too concerned with high-quality images—say, if you are posting fairly small-dimension images online—then mobile devices will be sufficient for many purposes. If you want to engage in higher-quality images or video outputs, such as photography for printed objects or the ability to capture video in lower-lighting situations, then you will need to go more in the direction of digital SLR cameras and higher-end camcorders. The ability to zoom and the amount of zoom that you have available with the camera are distinguishing factors, as is the speed of response from the camera, which can give you a clearer picture and a more stable image. Memory, which will generally be flash memory located within the camera, is another feature to watch for in an attempt to obtain the most you can with a device.

Audio-Recording/Editing Software

Software for recording sound will again vary depending on the purpose for the recording. Computers and tablets generally have built-in apps or software to capture audio recordings, or they have free or inexpensive options available for download. For example, Audacity is a free piece of software that runs on many devices and allows you to edit audio files. GarageBand is free software for MacOS and iOS devices that enables multitrack music recording and editing. In the middle ground, there are many inexpensive apps and software to download, such as Sony Sound Forge (Windows, Mac) or a nonprofit license for Reaper. For something a good bit pricier, Adobe Creative Suite includes a variety of software items to meet your media creation needs, including Adobe Audition for sound recording. Beyond the products mentioned here, if you are pursuing more serious music recording, you might want to explore more expensive recording and mixing software and equipment.

Image-Editing Software

A wide range of software is available to transform digital images. Very basic image editors come with all computer operating systems. There are freeware tools such as GIMP (GNU Image Manipulation Program) for Windows and Mac and Picasa for Windows, Mac, and Linux that can expand your capabilities in this area. Pixlr is a free app for Android and iOS devices; it is also a web-based image editor that can add effects and modify images. Pixelmator is a low-cost tool for Macs, and Corel PaintShop Pro is in a similar price range for Windows. Once again, on the more expensive side, you could consider Adobe Photoshop, which is part of Adobe Creative Suite, for more involved editing and overlaying of effects.

Video-Recording/Editing Software

MovieMaker (Windows) and iMovie (Mac) are included with their respective operating systems and will do the trick of editing video and combining audio with video. There are free web-based tools, such as WeVideo (which has an Android app), Animoto, and Lightworks (which can be downloaded for Windows and Linux). On the pricier end, you could buy Final Cut Pro for Mac or Adobe Premiere for Windows and Mac. As with all the various editors suggested in this section, it is best to try out some of the free resources and see if they can handle your needs, before you sink a significant sum of money into software that might see only occasional use.

Accessories

This catch-all category includes a range of items that can assist in media production. Microphones are often built into the devices mentioned previously, but there may be a need to add separate microphones, cabled or wireless, to meet your audio- and video-recording needs. Stand-alone digital audio recorders provide a mobile means for capturing audio, although this function is widely available in mobile devices. The more equipment that you add to a recording space, the more need you will have for stands to hold microphones and for tripods to hold cameras and other recording devices. Green screens are mentioned throughout this chapter, and they come in a variety of price points, from painted sheets that you can make yourself to portable screens that come with a stand. Lights are also useful to enhance the results of video production and photography. One other device that you might want to add to a computer is a scanner to convert printed images or other print matter into digital items.

Sliding Scale for Implementation

Here are three lists of items to add to a makerspace that can take on different levels of complexity in projects. There is also a document created by Joseph Sanchez (2013) that outlines a planning process for adding video, audio, and image technology to a library. On the basic end, you could get started with the following items.

Computer: Windows Desktop or iMac with 4–8 GB of RAM

Cameras: Point-and-shoot digital cameras, inexpensive camcorders, smartphones

Audio recording/editing: Audacity or other free editors

Image editing: GIMP or other free editors

Video/editing: MovieMaker or iMovie or other free editors

Accessories: Digital audio recorders, scanner

Taking it up a notch, you could add to (or replace) items from the previous list with these products:

Computer: Add additional RAM, increased hard drive or flash drive storage

Cameras: iPads or iPhones, higher-end camcorders

Audio recording/editing: Sony SoundForge

Image editing: Corel PaintShop Pro or Pixelmator

Video recording/editing: Final Cut Pro or Adobe Premiere Elements

Accessories: Microphones and stands, lighting kits for video production

Finally, you could work in some of the following items to add to your options and capabilities:

Computer: A dedicated Mac workstation (or multiple ones) for various media production needs, dedicated server space to archive and share digital files

Cameras: Digital SLR cameras

Audio recording/editing: Adobe Audition, Reaper, or Sound Forge Pro

Image editing: Adobe Photoshop

Video recording/editing: Adobe Premier

Accessories: A wide array of microphones for various needs, a large-bed scanner for scanning larger items

Refills Needed

Since so much of the capture, editing, production, and sharing of final products utilize device memory, hard drives, and cloud-based servers, there is not much to replace on a regular basis. There are blessedly fewer memory-holding media items (e.g., cassette tapes, CDs) to use that might get damaged or wear out from repeated use, except perhaps SD (secure digital) memory cards for some devices. The devices themselves will die out eventually, but so long as your patrons are relatively careful with them, you will not need replacements for a few years. You might need to replace microphones every now and then; likewise, you will need a supply of headphones or earbuds for people to use (or purchase) to listen to their creations in the larger library space.

Special Space Requirements and Options

Space for much of this form of making can be very flexible. Using a single tablet to capture sound and video and then edit that content and share it does not necessarily take much space at all. If you are going to work with props or animate objects, you will need a little room to spread things out while recording them. The same goes for working with a green screen or other backdrops for photography or video. Adding sound into the equation definitely pushes the dial toward "we need a room for this." In terms of not disturbing others in the library and, even if you have a separate room for a makerspace, not disturbing other makers or having them disturb you, sound projects tend to require some sort of quiet space to record.

You might already have some sort of flexible space in your library, such as a meeting room or study room that may be reserved for a sound- or video-recording session. Most of the equipment that you need can be quite mobile. If that sort of space is not available, then you should pursue converting some existing spot in the library into suitable space. It might be possible to turn an office or a closet into a recording studio without much expense, as the Smoky Hill Branch of the Arapahoe Library System did in Centennial, Colorado ("Arapahoe" 2013). You may need to pursue a larger renovation project, or you could purchase or construct a sound booth. A portable miniature one with instructions for building it is profiled on a website by Kooistra (2009).

⊚ Library Makerspace Profile: Penfield Library, State University of New York at Oswego, Oswego, NY

http://www.oswego.edu/library/learning_commons.html

Emily Thompson, Learning Technologies Librarian

How Did Your Makerspace Come to Be?

Library staff members were talking about problem-based learning and new theories of education and how they could support them. Students were being assigned multimedia projects and needed help with them. The library decided to reimagine a librarian job, and it hired Thompson to provide this assistance, rather than just hire technology-able student assistants.

The library does not have a separate location or area for the makerspace. Staff decided that libraries make scholarship; therefore, the whole library is the makerspace. Only two engineering degrees are offered on campus, so the library does not need a full-on tinkering space. Thompson wanted to add a 3D printer, since she believed that she could maintain it and that it would be used. The 3D printer and multimedia equipment have been very popular.

Thompson's approach to adding items to the makerspace and growing its services is to examine what the library already has and to suggest things that it might need. It is very much the same process that it uses for developing its library collection. Thompson has been able to use undesignated library funds to purchase equipment. She is able to add budget requests for consumable materials and new items to the library's technology services budget.

Who Uses It?

Thompson reports a variety of uses, both for the 3D printer and for other equipment. So far, she has printed a skull for a biology class and helped teams from another class create game pieces. Business majors needed to evaluate a stock, and they pretended that the Makerbot company was going to have an IPO. They came to the library in teams to see how the equipment worked and added that information to their profiles of the company.

The biggest users of the makerspace have been English students working on video projects and telling digital stories. The huge uptick of students has led to many appointments for Thompson. Students in a psychology class have also been active users during the last two semesters, now that their professor has replaced a final paper with a video project. Thompson assists students with various combinations of audio recordings with still images and video interviews. A psychology research methods course uses Prezi and PowerPoint extensively in videos. Animated projects are also popular with students, and many of them are new to the software.

Thompson has had the opportunity to make many presentations to classes on finding images using Creative Commons sources so that they are not stealing copyrighted items from the web. They have been interested to learn that they can seek out freely available versions of images so that they are not stealing.

How Do You Market the Makerspace?

Word of mouth has been extremely successful for letting people know about the makerspace. The library does post messages to the library's Facebook and Twitter accounts. It has held events to draw interest, such as one featuring games that SUNY Oswego students created using the 3D printer. Thompson's goal in her outreach efforts is to create connections with students that will lead them to try out the maker equipment. The library has an event in February where students make valentines, and she has used this opportunity to show the equipment and hold a petting zoo for students. She showed the Leap Motion 3D controller, iPads, and the 3D printer. She has also borrowed a robot from the campus's human computer interaction department to create interest. The library has raffled off iPod earbuds and free prints to students as prizes for this type of event.

Who Supports It?

Thompson provides the majority of support for the maker equipment at the moment. Most 3D printing that students do are from designs on Thingiverse.com, which require little modification, but she is starting to teach classes in 3D modeling that will give students the tools they need to change them. She is also adding a 3D scanner that will add more flexibility and possibilities. She is planning to hire a student to run jobs on the 3D printer, which will free some time up for her. Thompson currently relies on a reference tech squad that can answer many questions from students when she is otherwise engaged.

How Do You Stay Aware of Developments in Makerspaces?

Thompson has a Feedly (http://www.feedly.com) set up for technology updates from the blogs the Next Web (http://www.thenextweb.com) and ReadWrite (http://www.readwrite.com). She also looks at BoingBoing (http://www.boingboing.net) and sometimes Mashable (http://www.mashable.com) for ideas. She pays attention to what students are doing and what they are interested in. She has resigned herself to the fact that she cannot keep track of all the apps out there, but she is always coming up with new ideas and options. Thompson follows developments at the annual Consumer Electronics Show to see what new technologies might work for libraries.

What Do You See Happening in Your Makerspace in the Next Year?

The 3D scanner is definitely going into use in the coming semester. Makerbot (http://www.makerbot.com) keeps coming up with more ideas, and she expects to add more of its equipment. She will likely add more cameras; the library has 10 iPods now and 8 flip cameras, but the flip cameras are dying. She definitely would like to add more tripods.

A big focus ahead is to move the multimedia production room into a larger space. The current space experiences a hum from the electricity in other rooms nearby, and she needs to find a new space, though nothing is available now. Thompson would at least like to move the library's VHS-to-DVD converter to another area to make more room in the current space.

What Is Your Advice to Others Who Would Like to Create a Makerspace?

Have someone on staff who likes to take stuff apart. Machines require maintenance, and someone has to willing to deal with it. Repairs to the 3D printer and other items can be quick but require a lack of fear to open devices up. Thompson notes that the library provides wonderful customer service at Makerbot, but she advises that you need to be calm enough about the process to get through the fix. Overall, she recommends that you not depend on traditional library staff to take care of makerspace items but rather hire someone dedicated. Do not jump into more than you can handle with a makerspace implementation.

Thompson says that she hates to see rooms full of equipment that no one uses, and she suggests collaborating with others on campus who are interested in making activities or who have their own equipment. Know the demand that is out there before you pursue something. For instance, the library has a technology education department on campus with a really great shop. Because of this, the library decided that it did not need to add a lathe; it can just refer people to that unit rather than compete with it.

Thompson suggests a perspective on making that identifies the whole library as a makerspace. This has led to the location of making equipment in visible areas throughout the building, rather than taking over another space and possibly hiding the equipment. For marketing purposes, she recommends making things visible and available.

Her final words: "Take a risk but a calculated one."

⊚ Library Makerspace Profile: Western Academy of Beijing, Beijing, China

http://destiny.wab.edu/common/welcome.jsp?site=201

Jeri Hurd, Teacher-Librarian

How Did Your Makerspace Come to Be?

Hurd was eager to launch a makerspace in past positions but did not have the opportunity due to lacks of space and funding. Her current school has excellent technology resources and was open to the possibility. Hurd led an authoring project with history students in which they created chapters for an iBook from research that they completed on aspects of World War II. Following the project, she had students record videos discussing their work. The videos were so powerful that she and the teachers who were involved decided to make recording videos a more serious effort. They set up a studio with a couple of lights and a whiteboard for background. Students suddenly started to use the space on their own.

Hurd then talked up the idea of creating a makerspace, and she found that her administration was open to the idea. She attended a conference in Singapore and an "unconference" (participant-driven meeting) on makerspaces to learn more. She believed that the makerspace needed to be connected with the library because it is a space that is available to all students and cannot be tied to a certain discipline. The space is fairly small, able to fit only six people at a time. At the moment, the space is very film focused, but more is coming. This school is the only one in Beijing with a makerspace, which has impressed parents.

Funding has been managed from the library budget so far. Hurd bought cameras, lights, and backdrops to equip the current space but realizes that when she asks for more funds to expand, there might be an issue. The initial outlay of funds was between $4,000 and $5,000. Hurd posted her equipment list at http://www.scribd.com/doc/179096661/makerspace-equipment-pdf.

Who Uses It?

Hurd has a student "Geek Force" running the makerspace. The force is composed of 20 students who assist with a variety of technology activities at the school, and 6 of them are specifically assigned to work in the makerspace. They are providing training and workshops and helping out. They have already contributed ideas that she had not imagined for the space, and they are a very impressive group of kids. Hurd had the Geek Force show the capabilities of the space to teachers during an orientation, and the success of that effort left them feeling very empowered.

Since the high school offers an International Baccalaureate program, there are many required video projects that must be completed for the degree. The quality of these projects is not great so far, but students have just begun using the space, and Hurd imagines that they will improve with experience and new equipment. To date, Hurd has been surprised by the use of the space by students and teachers whom she did not expect would be interested.

How Do You Market the Makerspace?

The school is very technology forward as a whole, and there is great focus on getting students connected with technology. Hurd was able to get teachers on board and comfortable with using the makerspace during a 2-day professional development event. Every teacher had to complete a training session in the makerspace, conducted by Geek Force students. The hope was that the teachers would then bring their students along and assign projects that would necessitate use of the space.

How Do You Stay Aware of Developments in Makerspaces?

Hurd collects a variety of online resources on Scoop.it and regularly dumps new items in there for later review. She reads *Make:* magazine and is always looking for conferences that might offer other ideas or implementations. She mentioned how impressed she was with the makerspace at United World College in Singapore that she was able to visit during the conference that she attended.

What Do You See Happening in Your Makerspace in the Next Year?

Many good developments are planned for the coming year. The space itself will move into a larger space within the library, which will accommodate more students at one time.

Hurd is discussing expansion plans with design tech and art teachers to gather their input and find even more uses. One definite need is for art students to take videos of their sculptures and other creations to send to International Baccalaureate committees for grading. They will add robotics and coding activities and are planning to hold more workshops, with a focus on increasing student hands-on practice. A large-format printer will also be put in place, although Hurd says that she is not planning on expanding into items such as bandsaws. She would like to stick to items that do not require careful supervision while kids use them. She also plans to build a community of experts for workshops and troubleshooting needs by drawing parents with talents into the makerspace.

What Is Your Advice to Others Who Would Like to Create a Makerspace?

Hurd suggests starting where you are and building on to it. Do not wait for the perfect situation; do not work alone. She reached out to the school's technology integrator, who liked the idea and helped get it started. Hurd found it useful to get the school's technology people on board before approaching her administration. Now the buzz about the makerspace is building, and a wider group is starting to like the idea. Also, it is crucial to consider how the makerspace will affect student learning: what can students get out of this experience that they cannot do another way? Making the case for how the makerspace will influence students will go a long way toward justifying the investment.

⊚ Key Points

Working with images, audio, and video in the makerspace is a great way for patrons to learn skills and show their creativity. Another nice element about teaching these skills, apart from the individual talents that develop, is the ability for participants to then help chronicle what else is made in your makerspace.

- Producing media in a makerspace helps patrons become media creators and not just media consumers.
- Many audio, video, and image creation tools are becoming ubiquitous, but a makerspace can provide access to ones that not everyone will have.
- There are media creation tools available at multiple price points, and a library can enter into using them along a sliding scale of options.

Next, the creativity continues with crafts and artistic creations in chapter 7.

⊚ References

"Arapahoe Library Lets Patrons Borrow Recording Studio." 2013. 9News.com. February 3. http://www.9news.com/news/local/article/314508/346/Arapahoe-Library-lets-patrons-borrow-recording-studio.

Jenkins, Henry, Sam Ford, and Joshua Green. 2013. *Spreadable Media: Creating Value and Meaning in a Networked Culture*. New York: New York University Press.

Kooistra, Durk. 2009. "Portable Mini Vocal Booth." Humanworkshop. August 15. http://humanworkshop.com/index.php?modus=e_zine&sub=articles&item=115.

Quinn, Brendan. 2013. "Collaboration, Teaching, and Technology in Northwestern University Library's Digital Collections Training Lab." In *The New Academic Librarian: Essays on Changing Roles and Responsibilities*, edited by Rebecca Peacock and Jill Wurm, 161–69. Jefferson, NC: McFarland & Company.

Sanchez, Joseph. 2013. "From Content Warehouse to Content Provider: Libraries at the Crossroads." http://www.thebookmyfriend.com/uploads/6/1/1/3/6113160/from_content_warehouse_to_content_producer_libraries_at_the_crossroads.pdf.

CHAPTER 7

Resources for Crafts and Artistic Pursuits

IN THIS CHAPTER

▷ Made by Hand

▷ Made by Machines

▷ Arts and Crafts Making in the Survey

▷ What Your Patrons Could Be Making

▷ Tools for Craft and Artistic Pursuits Projects

▷ Refills Needed

▷ Special Space Requirements and Options

▷ Library Makerspace Profile: College of San Mateo Library, San Mateo, CA

▷ Library Makerspace Profile: Chicago Ridge Public Library, Chicago Ridge, IL

MAKING IN LIBRARIES CAN INVOLVE ARTS AND CRAFTS—traditional hand-made items and machine-created or machine-aided constructions. The projects can involve final products that are purely artistic or ones that also serve practical purposes. "Arts and crafts" is a fairly inclusive concept, and it will be employed in this chapter to bookend a variety of different activities. From serving as easy entry points for the act of making to enabling patrons to use equipment to create detailed items, work with arts and crafts activities can be a vital part of a makerspace.

◎ Made by Hand

An interesting facet of arts and crafts in makerspaces is that there are easy entry points and the ability to gain expertise whether you are producing something by hand or using a programmed machine. Makerspaces can feature traditional forms of crafting, such as origami, sewing, or carving; they can also have laser cutters and automated sewing machines. The handmade crafts are ones that can be taken on by amateurs of any age. They are appealing opportunities to offer to anyone who is interested in making something that does not require a huge investment in materials and equipment. This might cut against the idea that library makerspaces can offer (or maybe should only offer) making opportunities that patrons cannot afford on their own. But handmade crafts are not without a requirement for instruction and a need for community support that a makerspace can provide, nor are they necessarily without mess that might keep someone from trying it at home. Combining the ease of entry, the draw toward community, and the satisfaction of completing something with hands and hand tools makes these tasks well fit to the makerspace ethic.

◎ Made by Machine

As rewarding as it can be to build objects by hand, it is also exciting to see the technological aspect of makerspaces at work in machine-aided crafts. In addition to traditional hand use of sewing machines or woodworking equipment, machines are being used to create items through human programming. Computer numerical control (CNC) devices and laser and vinyl cutters can cut, etch, stitch, and otherwise transform many types of materials following a programmed pattern. They provide the ability to create intricate designs and precise lines and curves that can be difficult for the human eye and hand. The relative ease of creating and adapting patterns and the reduced entry price for this equipment make this an exciting option for making.

◎ Arts and Crafts Making in the Survey

The informal library makerspace survey provides a sense of the scope of these activities in library makerspaces. Several of the 55 technologies and activities listed in the survey cover the content of this chapter. The broader term *art and crafts* was chosen as an activity in 40 of the 109 libraries (37 percent of all libraries responding). More specific areas of creation included activities related to fabric and sewing (18 libraries, 17 percent), laser cutting (9 libraries, 8 percent), large format printer (9 libraries, 8 percent), vinyl cutting (8 libraries, 7 percent), and screen printing (5 libraries, 5 percent). Smaller groups of libraries chose woodworking (4 libraries, 4 percent), ceramics, CNC machines, and jewelry making (3 libraries, 3 percent for each of the last three activities). One or two libraries listed each of the following technologies or activities: industrial sewing machine, milling machine, mold making, potter's wheel and kiln, and silk screening. All told, the activities collected here under arts and crafts totaled 109 of the 956 choices of technologies and activities in the survey, or 11 percent.

The survey results lead nicely into a discussion of what these technologies and activities are and what patrons could do with them in a makerspace environment. There is a wide variety of categories of making that could be covered in a chapter on arts and crafts in makerspaces. This one focuses on some approaches and media that you could work with and the equipment that you might need.

Upcycling

A popular approach to arts and crafts in a makerspace is upcycling, or reusing discarded items. This can connect with an environmentally friendly focus among your patrons; it also reduces the cost of many applications. It might involve changing the purpose of the item, such as filling plastic or glass bottles or containers with dirt and plants to make terrariums. Or it might involve transforming the item by using just part of it or combining multiple discarded items for a new purpose, such as turning old pillows into a dog bed (Richardson 2013). The two examples given so far are fairly practical ones, but there are also applications for upcycling in fashion and in art. Many fashionable examples can come from a single long-sleeved shirt: buttons, a headband, a carrying case, doll clothes, and napkins (Sparkleponytx 2014). On the artistic side, you could create a chandelier with an old trout net and some discarded glass bottles (ClaudineK 2014). Many options are possible with upcycling, and it can be a sustainable part of the other types of crafting in this chapter.

Paper

Paper-related creation can take a variety of forms. Given the description of upcycling, the paper involved can include scrap paper or leftovers from a project. Paper-folding methods such as origami can create 3D figures that can run the range from fairly simple shapes to intricate designs (see figure 7.1 for an example). Patrons working on scrapbooks can blend multiple pieces of paper to highlight photos with intricate or distinctive borders. Collages can be created with plain-colored paper or by combining images from discarded periodicals. Posters and signs can be created by etching words or images with a vinyl cutter, drawing on paper either freehand or with stencils, printed from word processing or other software, or even screen printed or silk screened onto paper with ink and a stencil. You can use paper to prototype various things, such as building methods, by rolling or stacking folded paper to test the durability of a design or aerodynamic concepts (with your old friend the paper airplane). Papier-mâché transforms old newspapers into creations large and small with the application of paste, supports, and time to dry. Paper is a flexible medium that can also be fairly easy to store.

Sewing/Fabrics

Another popular medium is fabric. Sewing can provide both artistic and practical projects for fabric. It is a skill that can be used to create new clothing, accessories, and other items and to repair existing ones. Sewing can be done by hand or with a sewing machine that

Figure 7.1. Papercraft R2-D2. *Image provided through a CC BY 2.0 License by Kristen Stubbs, http:// www.flickr.com/photos/kristenstubbs/3882056033*

is human directed and operated (see figure 7.2). There are also specialty machines called *sergers*, which are useful for sewing and cutting the edges of fabric products so that they do not unravel. Taking the machinery a step further, there are CNC sewing machines that can create sewn items from a program. Sewing is a popular activity at the Chicago Ridge Public Library (profiled later in this chapter), Anythink Brighton (profiled in chapter 4), and the Richland Library (profiled in chapter 3). It is interesting to think of the longevity

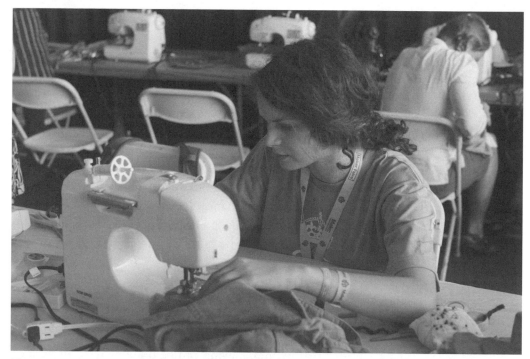

Figure 7.2. Sewing at the maker faire. *Image provided through a CC BY 2.0 License by Jon Callas (joncallas), http://www.flickr.com/photos/joncallas/7230408600*

of sewing, given that it features in some of the earliest examples of making in libraries, going back to 1877 ("A History of Making" 2013).

There are many opportunities for upcycling unused or discarded fabric. Screen-printing or silk-screening fabric allows it to take on an image, words, or a complete design. Any making activity involving fabric requires that it be cut, often to precise dimensions to ensure a perfect outcome. Equipment such as laser cutters (which use a laser to burn through fabric) or vinyl cutters (which use a blade) can be programmed to cut exact patterns to ensure a consistent outcome. Fabric can be stuffed to make pillows, dolls, and a whole host of other possibilities beyond clothing. There are many plans and ideas for fabric at Instructables.com (http://instructables.com) if you search under the terms *fabric*, *clothing*, or another specific need.

Needlework

It would not be proper to talk of sewing in makerspaces without adding in needlework crafts such as knitting, crocheting, and quilting, which make use of yarn and thread to create items. Groups formed to work on these activities have met in some public libraries for many years. They may work on a large cooperative project, such as a quilt, in which each member contributes a square; they may also gather to encourage one another as they make individual projects. Now, these individuals can be makers that pass their crafts on to other patrons who are new to needlework. For some people, crocheting can be very exciting, as evidenced by the experience that the Michigan Makers had in teaching this skill in an elementary school (see the profile in chapter 5). There may also be opportunities to combine low-tech needlework with technology, such as placing LED lights that come on in sequence within a quilt that is hung in the library (Barone 2014).

Metal, Wood, and More

Working with more substantial media may not be for every library makerspace. Metal and wood tend to require more equipment and less mobile equipment than the prior media. As covered here, they may well be noisy and messy and require dedicated spaces. But some of these issues vary in severity depending on what you plan to do with metal, wood, vinyl, plastics, and other substances. Hand carving and assembly of wood with glue, hammer, and nail or wire sculpture projects completed with hand tools are not especially messy or loud. But welding a metal frame or using a CNC cutting machine or table saw to cut a piece of wood takes this to another level, in terms of the impact on others in the general area and on heightened needs for safety and training.

Notwithstanding these issues, there are some wonderful building and creating opportunities afforded by pursuing these crafts. Wood can be turned into everything from napkin holders to planter boxes (KevinB 2013). Metal strips can be cut and then engraved with logos, barcodes, or QR codes by a laser cutter ("Logo and Barcode" 2014). You can even cast metal objects using a mold that you design and cut out of cardboard using a laser cutter (Lucylollipop 2014). There is more coverage of the use of plastic in 3D printing in chapter 9, but there are other plastic projects, such as a bird feeder made from a plastic bottle (Koningsbrugge 2014). Another possible project is jewelry creating, which can be made from materials other than wood or metal but can have impressive results when these media are chosen.

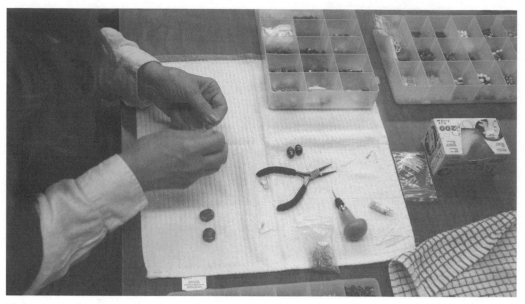

Figure 7.3. Jewelry making at the College of San Mateo Library. *Provided by Katherine Becvar*

Jewelry

Jewelry is another popular product of makerspaces, with many projects available on the Instructables.com site (do a search for *jewelry* to have a sense of the breadth of options). Jewelry can be constructed from wood, metal, or plastic, using laser cutters, woodworking tools, and soldering kits. But jewelry can also be made by hand from beads, shells, ribbons, lengths of cord, and other items. See figure 7.3 for some sample products.

Ceramics

Creating artistic and useful objects from clay is another possibility for the library makerspace. Ceramics involve the shaping of an item from clay and then heating the clay to harden it. Makers can create figurines, tiles, pots, mugs, coasters, key chains, jewelry, and all sorts of other items. Again, a search of Instructables.com for *ceramics* will provide many examples of projects to pursue. Items can be shaped by hand or with handheld tools, or a spinning potter's wheel can be used to shape pots, vases, and other cylindrical items. A kiln is an ovenlike device that can properly heat items to harden them. It is a serious investment in ceramics.

Tools for Craft and Artistic Pursuits Projects

Here are some makerspace items that you will want to have in place to take on the making ideas from this chapter.

CNC Machines

CNC machines can follow programmed patterns to cut, shape, and even sew materials (figure 7.4). They require a connection to a computer to work and a design programmed in CAD software (Kemp 2013, 206). Long present in large-scale industrial applications, this

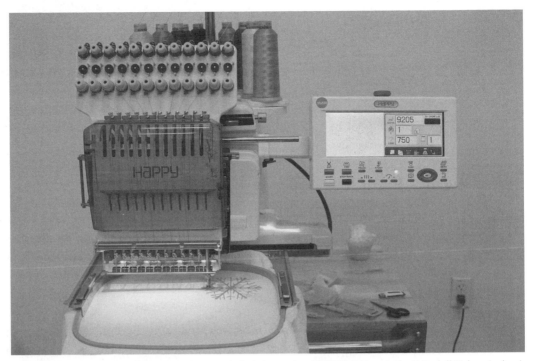

Figure 7.4. CNC Snowflakes 1. *Image provided through a CC BY 2.0 License by Windell Oskay (oskay), http://www.flickr.com/photos/oskay/8305280825*

equipment can now be used more easily by interested individuals due to the availability of smaller and less expensive units, the creation of open sources for patterns, and a growing community of users. In an environment where you want to give patrons the ability to create designs and then produce precisely cut or sewn pieces, CNC machines provide an exciting opportunity.

Laser Cutters

Precision cutting and engraving are also possible with a laser cutter, which uses a focused laser beam on wood, glass, metal, paper, plastic, and many fabrics at the direction of a CAD-designed pattern. There are different types of lasers to choose from depending on the application that you have in mind, and Kemp offers some guidelines (2013, 182–83). Since the laser effectively melts the material, there can be harmful fumes produced, and some materials may not be suitable for laser cutting ("Laser Cutter" 2013). Inkscape and Adobe Illustrator are commonly used to create designs, but other CAD programs can be used.

Vinyl Cutters

A vinyl cutter has some similarity to the laser cutter but also some key differences. It is computer driven, following a pattern to cut items. It uses a blade rather than a laser, which limits the materials that it can cut. It can handle paper of various kinds and vinyl sheets to produce signs and decals. Software such as Adobe Illustrator and Inkscape or software included with the cutter is needed to input designs and send them to the cutter. Vinyl cutters come in various sizes, with desktop models available for smaller jobs (Chang 2013).

Die Cut Machines

With the focus so far on computer-guided cutting devices, hand-operated cutters should not be forgotten. Die cut machines can cut specialized shapes for which dies are created. The die presses into paper that is added to the machine to create multiple copies of the shape. This equipment can be useful in various paper-related making activities, including scrapbooking and sign making. AccuCut and Ellison are leading brands of die cutting machines.

Large-Format Printer

Large-format printers are useful for printing large posters and signs. Depending on the printer, they can print to paper sizes that are double the width of standard paper (from 8.5 × 11 in. to 11 × 17 in.), or they can print from rolled paper at a width of 36 in.

Sewing Machines

Apart from the CNC sewing machines already discussed, human-operated sewing machines are of interest for makerspaces that feature fabrics. Many choices of machines are available, but one consideration to make is where the sewing machines will be used. If they will be transported to various locations or moved from storage into use on a regular basis, a portable machine will be preferable.

Soldering and Welding

Soldering kits can be a useful addition to the makerspace for metal-joining purposes. This might be helpful for metal sculpture making or jewelry creation in the arts and crafts area, but they will also be helpful for use in electronics, as discussed in chapter 8. Soldering consists of using a heat source to melt metallic filler that is then placed between two metal items. As the filler hardens, the two items are joined. Welding, however, requires using a heat source that melts the metal on the two pieces that you wish to join, in addition to an added filler. Welding is definitely stepping up a notch in terms of the size of the materials that can be joined and the level of safety that is required to operate the equipment. Welding will be added to the makerspace only if the nature of the work going on there requires that level of equipment. It also requires certification to be able to handle the equipment.

Hand Tools

A variety of hand tools may be useful for the various functions described in this chapter. For most of the arts and crafts activities described here, pliers and scissors are essential items to have for the successful completion of the creation. Note that having multiple pairs of scissors and pliers for instructional sessions should not be forgotten.

Refills Needed

There are many consumable items in the activities described in this chapter. Fabric, yarn, paper, glue, metal, wood, clay, and other items will need to be regularly added to the makerspace to keep projects running. Blades will need to be sharpened and regular maintenance performed on equipment. The key thing will be to keep track of supplies and to budget for specific projects. With regular use, the needed supplies will be easier to estimate.

◎ Special Space Requirements and Options

This area of creation has probably the widest range of considerations for space depending on the medium and equipment that are chosen. Several paper, wood, and vinyl-cutting crafts could be performed anywhere with minimal setup or precautions. But more complex and involved activities and use of larger equipment will necessitate dedicated spaces and additional time and practice requirements to succeed in safe making practice. What follow are key aspects to consider about space arrangement and preparation with these activities.

Safety

The dangerous nature of cutting and welding equipment requires makerspaces to have the means to separate these items from patrons who are not working on them. Makerspace participants will also need a certification process to prove that they are trained in using such equipment: sometimes a formal certification, at other times the makerspace's own rules to "certify" that someone is ready to use something.

Noise and Dirty Space

Many pieces of equipment are loud and create a lot of waste materials (sawdust, metal shavings, etc.). Even cutting and sewing fabric can leave threads and scraps behind. Those planning the makerspace need to realistically assess how well these issues can be addressed in the space chosen in the library. Occasional noise issues could probably be dealt with for a mobile makerspace holding a workshop here or there. Likewise, the dirty space requirements could be met, but in both cases, if a more regular level of activity is expected (e.g., an open lab), then dedicated space with noise reduction capabilities will be needed.

Electricity

For some of the paper or handwork wood crafts, electricity may not be a consideration. But most activities described will require electricity for computers and other pieces of equipment. Hopefully, no one will buy a CNC lathe without thinking out where it will fit in the library and whether there are enough outlets available. But even as the Chicago Ridge Public Library found, it can be hard to find enough outlets to keep 16 small sewing machines running. Careful examination of the needs and the location will help address this issue.

Room to Spread Out Materials and Equipment

All the activities discussed in this chapter would benefit from having enough space and furniture available to spread out materials and equipment so that materials can be placed, measured, and otherwise prepared for the next steps in the process. This is a common need for activities in the library makerspace.

Figure 7.5. Soldering workshop at the College of San Mateo Library. *Provided by Katherine Becvar*

Ventilation

Many examples of cutting equipment and any operations involving the soldering or welding of materials will require that ventilation be provided to remove toxic fumes from the space (figure 7.5). This will be something to look into as you are considering purchasing equipment and placing it in the library.

◎ Library Makerspace Profile: College of San Mateo Library, San Mateo, CA

http://collegeofsanmateo.edu/library/makerspace.php

Katherine Becvar, Adjunct Librarian

How Did Your Makerspace Come to Be?

Becvar got into a conversation about the growing trend of makerspaces in libraries with Lorrita Ford, the library director, and they started exploring the possibility of starting a makerspace at the College of San Mateo Library. Becvar owns a costume and sewing business and is an artist in addition to her work as a librarian. Ford and Becvar applied for on-campus funding through a president's grant intended to fund innovative programs for serving students in new ways. The library was awarded $7,000 and started up maker activities in April 2013, including jewelry making, "yarn bombing" (a type of street art), and book binding. They were also loaned a 3D printer from the college's engineering club. So far, they have focused on offering workshops and organizing making activities. Becvar and her colleagues also reached out to faculty and asked them to teach workshops, often discovering talents that they had beyond what they normally teach. This fits in with a component of the maker movement about showing off skills and sharing skills with others. Suggestions from students have also inspired activities.

They have been conservative about expenses so far and not purchased any large fabrication equipment, such as 3D printers, scanners, or laser cutters. Becvar said that they wanted to see what will resonate with students first, since it would be a shame to invest in something that just sits around unused. Instead, they have bought pliers, soldering irons, paper, and "old school" craft materials, such as glue and scissors. The response so far has worked really well with a smaller investment. As their needs increase, they are open to adding more equipment. They are applying for additional money through same grant program for a 3D printer and either a Silhouette cutter or a scanner. They are also exploring other funding possibilities.

Becvar stressed the need to start to build a community of makers first and then decide what stuff to put in the makerspace. She compared it to a reference collection: what works in one library might not fit another. There are so many different kinds of equipment and materials that can support a makerspace, and you will not know what your makers are interested in making until you start asking them. The makerspace should reflect its community.

Who Uses It?

Students, staff, and professors have regularly come to participate in workshops. The experience is really creating a community of peers in that faculty and staff members are often learning from students. Their community college's students have a wide diversity of career goals, ranging from firefighters to cosmetologists, as well as people working to transfer to 4-year schools. The institution is trying to help students make academic connections. It wants to see students excited about their own learning processes, and working on maker activities brings this out.

The library is developing the makerspace organically. In the fall of 2013, Becvar and her colleagues started to see students take leadership roles and set a direction for the makerspace. Participation in the activities has been cross disciplinary, with representatives from engineering, art, and the fashion club.

How Do You Market the Makerspace?

Makerspace workshops are listed on the campus events calendar and are advertised with flyers and posters around campus. Word-of-mouth advertising has worked well. They also send a few e-mails out to students, although the campus restricts how many are sent to students. They are doing a lot of surveys of workshop attendees to see what their interests are. They are trying to get survey responses from every workshop attendee, and then this information can be used to focus outreach toward them. There are many clubs on campus, and a regular interclub council meeting on campus provides a chance to market activities and get clubs to cosponsor workshops. Announcements are also made using the library's Facebook page and Twitter account and on the library website.

How Do You Stay Aware of Developments in Makerspaces?

Becvar has been a *Make:* magazine subscriber for a long time and gets a lot of ideas for workshop activities from the *Make:* blog. Becvar has been attending the Bay Area

Maker Faire for several years. She also hears about developments from within her artistic community. She has found that electronic discussion lists have not always been useful as passive information sources. For instance, a K–12 Fab Labs discussion that she read was not very helpful, but it was great to turn to the list when she had a question.

What Do You See Happening in Your Makerspace in the Next Year?

A baseline plan for the coming year is to create a makerspace club to keep maker activities sustainable. Given the 2-year tenure of students on campus, it is important to have a way to transfer the maker culture from one semester to the next. Given the number of clubs on campus, creating one for the makerspace will, ideally, help it fit it into campus life.

In terms of what Becvar might hope for or dream about, she would like to see faculty incorporate hands-on learning in their class assignments and then make the makerspace part of their class instruction. She would also like to have students working on longer-term projects and using the library space as a continuous work space.

What Is Your Advice to Others Who Would Like to Create a Makerspace?

Get started. Start talking about it. Start with something basic and get people interested. You do not need equipment or specialized knowledge in the beginning. You might be really surprised to see what develops. It does not take much to cultivate interest and enthusiasm for making.

⊚ Library Makerspace Profile: Chicago Ridge Public Library, Chicago Ridge, IL

http://www.chicagoridgelibrary.org

Kathy McSwain, Library Director

How Did Your Makerspace Come to Be?

For 11 years, a quilting group has met in the library: the Block of the Month program. It began with a member of the group bringing in a sewing machine each month and demonstrating how to make a quilting square. Then members would go home and quilt, returning each month from September to May to learn a new block, and show the completed block from the prior month. The program grew very popular, with more and more people joining to learn how to quilt. The Illinois State Library had Library Services and Technology Act grants available for emerging technologies in 2006, and McSwain applied for one. After doing research and getting pricing, she wrote a grant to buy 16 sewing machines: lightweight Janome Jems, 12 pounds each. The library also bought an AccuCut die cutting machine and additional dies to cut fabric.

As part of the grant proposal, they taught groups of Girl Scout troops how to quilt for a 2-week period. The troops came to the library and learned how to sew, make blocks, and create hotpads. A couple of the troops returned to the library to make blankets for charity and to outfit their Girl Scout cabin. There were a total of 18 quilting sessions serving 197 Girl Scouts and 33 leaders at the time of the grant.

Who Uses It?

The sewing machines have been very popular and work well. They are still in use today. The library moved to offer quilting classes and hired a quilter or two to lead them. The classes drew some of the regular Block of the Month quilters but also added new patrons to the quilting ranks. Now they have lock-ins on the last Friday of the month (except in November and December and the summer months) from 6 PM to 11 PM. There is just an open room for quilters, knitters, and crocheters. In addition, a patron has attended with photographs to make a collage. That made a lot of the attendees curious and really drew them in.

The groups of crafters keep these making activities going. McSwain is a crafty, creative person and really likes to try out different crafts. She also maintains the sewing machines and said that they are easy to thread. There is a hard-core group of 20 quilters and a dozen knitters and crocheters who come to the monthly meetings and then return during the week to work on their projects. Some ladies just come in and meet in a study room to sew. The knitters and crocheters are known as the Needle Maniacs. There is also a retired youth services librarian who collects dolls, and she meets with her doll group in the library monthly to show off dolls and accessories. They have a mixture of historic ones and collectible ones, along with more modern and interesting ones. They have been meeting at the library for 5 or 6 years.

How Do You Market the Makerspace?

The classes and equipment are mentioned in the library newsletter. New quilting groups start up each September with a new Block of the Month plan. The person who teaches the class comes up with the pattern and makes it easy for new people to join, even if they have limited experience. There is also a stampers group that stamps and makes cards or gift bags with the AccuCut machine. Some of them are knitters as well, but most are just stampers. They do create interest in their projects through show-and-tell opportunities. These conversations really get people interested in stamping.

What Do You See Happening in Your Makerspace in the Next Year?

The library just started a painting program in September and October 2013. An artist in town volunteered to offer the program and bought easels, canvases, and paint. There was a small charge to participate. Twenty attendees learned how to move their brushes to represent a vase of lilacs on the canvas. This led to two more painting parties, and the work done by participants included simple paintings, though quite beautiful, and really encouraged the new artists to continue. There will be more painting in the year ahead. One man wanted to display his work in the library, and that helped promote the classes. This tied in well with the annual display of knitting work that they place in the library around Christmas time. People enjoy looking at the work and sometimes purchase items. In the summer, the library also has charity quilting events to create quilts and table runners and then sell them for charity donation.

In addition to the quilting, knitting, and sewing, the library also hosts a garden club that meets regularly. It will bring in a master gardener to give advice and answer questions. It also regularly brings in a chef to talk about canning and fast freezing.

McSwain is hoping to create some larger rooms in the library that allow for larger groups to meet. Right now, it has a study room with a gigantic table and 10 chairs. It works fine for the doll club, but it is not usable by the quilters or other groups. Moving forward, McSwain hopes to rework spaces and create new spaces with flexible furniture. Also, she would like to add more comfortable furniture for the knitters.

What Is Your Advice to Others Who Would Like to Create a Makerspace?

The key element is making sure that you have space, not only to do the programs, but also to store the equipment. The library stores a bin of materials for the knitters and keeps the sewing machines on two book carts so that they can be rolled out to available space. It also has big cutting mats and rulers for the AccuCut and other equipment, and it has added surge protectors to space the sewing machines on tables near outlets. Having sufficient power available to keep the equipment running is so crucial. The library also gets donations of yarn, which require a lot of storage space. McSwain reports that she keeps the AccuCut machine in her office, which can get in her way, but she loves having it.

In her 38 years in libraries, McSwain has witnessed many changes. She has seen a lot of progress and knows that there is still a long way to go. She stresses that the library is all about teaching skills beyond reading and providing story hours.

◎ Key Points

In considering adding arts and crafts activities to your makerspace, here are some key items to remember:

- Arts and crafts making activities can take a wide variety of forms and levels of complexity.
- Handmade making and machine-assisted making are both very challenging and can turn out equally beautiful creations.
- An exciting element of makerspace arts and crafts is the precision and speed added by technology that brings the capability of making these items to a wider audience of makers.

Now on to forms of making that are less physical and even more dependent on technology, in all of its aspects, in the next chapter.

◎ References

Barone, Meg. 2014. "High-Tech Quilting Project Knits Together Westport Community." West-Port-News.com. January 20. http://www.westport-news.com/news/article/High-tech-quilting-project-knits-together-5158843.php.

Chang, Stephanie. 2013. "Three Transformative Tools: From Old Tech to New (Part 2)." *Makezine* (blog). July 16. http://makezine.com/2013/07/16/three-transformative-tools-from-old-tech-to-new-part-2/.

ClaudineK. 2014. "Upcycled Chandelier." Instructables.com. http://www.instructables.com/id/Upcycled-Chandelier/.

"A History of Making." 2013. *American Libraries* 44 (1/2): 46.

Kemp, Adam. 2013. *The Makerspace Workbench: Tools, Technologies, and Techniques for Making*. Sebastopol, CA: Maker Media.

KevinB. 2013. "Weekend Project: Planter Boxes!" MilwaukeeMakerspace.org. June 14. http://milwaukeemakerspace.org/2013/06/weekend-project-planter-boxes/.

Koningsbrugge, Ruud van. 2014. "Plastic Bottle Birdhouse." Instructables.com. http://www.instructables.com/id/Plastic-bottle-birdhouse/.

"Laser Cutter." 2013. Robots and Dinosaurs Hackerspace (wiki). July 8. http://hackerspace.pbworks.com/w/page/41180361/Lasercutter.

"Logo and Barcode Marked Aluminum." 2014. MELDWorkshop.com. http://meldworkshop.com/projects/logo-and-barcode-marked-aluminum.

Lucylollipop. 2014. "Metal Casting." Instructables.com. http://www.instructables.com/id/Metal-Casting/.

Richardson, Greg. 2013. "$6 Upcycled Dog Bed." *7hills Makerspace* (blog). October 12. http://7hillsmake.org/2013/10/12/6-upcycled-dog-bed/.

Sparkleponytx. 2014. "5 Things to Do with an Old Shirt." Instructables.com. http://www.instructables.com/id/5-Things-to-Do-with-An-Old-Shirt/.

CHAPTER 8

Resources for Electronics, Robotics, and Programming

THREE VERY INTRIGUING FORMS OF MAKING are contained in the topics of electronics, robotics, and programming. Makers working with these tools and activities are interested in making things happen, whether through constructing electrical devices; creating robots or other devices that people can watch, control, or interact with; or bringing websites and mobile apps into being with programming. There is a lot of interplay in these activities as well, in which an assembled device can be automated through programming. There are also lots of easy entry points for new makers to learn electrical and programming concepts that they, along with more advanced users, can use to create interesting and practical devices and services. This chapter examines technologies and activities that a makerspace can provide to encourage and support work with electronics, robotics, and programming.

⊚ Electronics, Robotics, and Programming in the Survey

First, a review of the informal survey results can provide a sense of the scope of these activities in library makerspaces (see the appendix for details). The content of this chapter figured in 29 percent of the choices made from the list of 55 technologies and activities in the survey (279 of the 956 total choices). At the top of the list was the category of computer programming and software, yielding 43 choices from the 109 respondents (39 percent). In the next most common category, 37 makerspaces (34 percent) featured programming and software to create websites or online portfolios. Next came Arduino and Raspberry Pi microcontrollers, which are present in 33 of the makerspaces (30 percent). Moving down the list, creating apps and games were each chosen by 24 respondents (22 percent). Electronics was chosen by 23 respondents (21 percent), and robotics was chosen by 19 (17 percent). Hacking circuits was found in 17 makerspaces (16 percent), and digital scrapbooking appeared in 16 (15 percent). The final three were soft circuits and electronic book production, each with 15 responses (14 percent), and mobile development with 13 (12 percent). Ranking the activities and technologies by the percentage of libraries that have them is not meant to connote their value or across-the-board acceptance in library makerspaces. It does show that each has a solid place in multiple libraries. Some of the interactions among them are explored as the types of making are discussed here.

⊚ What Your Patrons Could Be Making

To further explore the broad categories and specific items in the survey results, here is a selection of activities that are practiced in makerspaces involving electronics, robotics, and programming. Consider this a starting point for possibilities in this area.

Making Stuff to Learn about Electronics

Makers who are new to electronics can utilize kits and sets to learn how things work. More on these in a moment, but there are even more elemental and inexpensive ways to practice working with electronic devices. A great example of this is building an LED throwie: a small colorful LED light, a 3V lithium battery, and some tape. Just tape the LED onto the battery, and you have a throwie (named because you can throw it up in the air at night and enjoy the effect). Add a magnet, and your light will stick to surfaces. Add a piece of cardstock, and you can fold it so that it breaks contact between the LED and the battery, serving as an on/off switch (Hammond 2013). Add . . . well, as you can see, this pretty simple and cheap experiment (around a dollar) can build in complexity and create interest. Figure 8.1 gives you an idea of what these look like.

Now back to the kits and sets. There are a variety of products available to help introduce children and people of any age who are new to electronics. Examples of these include littleBits, which offer sets of modules that snap together with magnets. The modules are little circuit boards that serve as connectors, buzzers, switches, pressure sensors, and other elements that can be found in electronic circuitry. By combing the modules with household items such as paper, boxes, tape, LEGOs, and other items, you can create such projects as talking cereal boxes (with flapping tongues) and seascape scenes with moving construction paper waves, and you can trick out your skateboard with programmed

Figure 8.1. IMG_0461. *Image provided through a CC BY 2.0 License by urban_data, http://www. flickr.com/photos/urban_data/438642086*

lights (see the examples at http://littlebits.cc/projects or on the Instructables.com site by searching "littleBits"). Along the way, littleBits makers are learning how circuitry works and building up skills to make more complex projects.

A couple of similar products are Snap Circuits and Squishy Circuits. Snap Circuits consist of plastic and metal parts that you lay out on a plastic board. Once they are connected and linked in a circuit, some sort of activity ensues, depending on which components you have added. You can create motion detectors, lights with light switches, various sound-producing items, and even mobile items once you take the circuits from the plastic board and mount them on a vehicle (see more examples at http://www.snap-circuits.net/learning_center/kids_creation or on the Instructables.com site by searching "snap circuits"). Squishy Circuits can teach the same skills and produce similar products as these but with the addition of dough. The dough conducts electricity, and the recipe for which is freely available at http://courseweb.stthomas.edu/apthomas/SquishyCircuits/. It can be used to link lights, switches, and other electrical items. It is an appealing medium for children to use in these projects because it is one that they are already familiar with (Thomas 2013). Sample projects are available at the website cited or on YouTube.com (just search for "squishy circuits").

The main distinctions among the three products are options, cost, and ease of use. LittleBits are more expandable and flexible in terms of the prebuilt modules that they have available and the way that they connect with magnets, but they are more expensive. Snap Circuits are easy to work with for even younger kids but have a more limited array of projects. Squishy Circuits can be the least expensive in that the dough recipe is freely available and you are responsible only for providing the electronic components, LEDs, or wires that you add into the dough.

Making Stuff Go

Once the process of connecting electrical components is understood, another activity to pursue is devices that make things happen. The happening can be fairly simple, such as lights that blink, or very involved, such as a robot that can alter its movement in response to the placement of furniture or people who cross its path. These devices, known as microcontrollers, require not only the connection of circuits and devices but also the addition of programming to the equation. Programming allows these devices to operate automatically and independently so that no one has to throw a switch or hold a wire on a battery, as in the earlier electronic examples. What follow are some components that might be used to create projects in this way.

Arduino

Arduinos are little devices that provide a link between hardware (e.g., light sensors, lights, and motors) and the software program that directs the hardware. See figure 8.2 to get an idea of what one is. It is a circuit board that you can plug components into, but it also has the ability to be programmed. It can hold one program, or sketch, at a time. There is a whole library of open-source sketches available that you can use "as is" or adapt to your specific need and to the components that you are going to use. So, you can use a USB cable to connect the Arduino to a computer and then use free Arduino Development Environment software to enter your commands and compile and upload the sketch (O'Neill and Williams 2014). Then you unplug the Arduino, and it is ready to do whatever you told it to do in the sketch. What can you do with it? Well, you can create some

Figure 8.2. Raspberry Pi Model B und Arduino Uno. *Image provided through a CC BY 2.0 License by redcctshirt, http://www.flickr.com/photos/redcctshirt/10192600203*

incredible light shows with flashing lights, a rotating globe, and a self-controlled vehicle. There are many interesting possibilities on the Arduino website (http://www.arduino.cc) and Instructables.com (http://instructables.com). Books such as the ones by Melgar and Diez (2012) and Kemp (2013) can also lead you into interesting applications beyond the basics. Something that you may find the need for with the Arduino and other electronic projects is a breadboard, which is a piece of plastic with little plug holes in it where you can connect electronic devices without having to solder them together. It is meant as a temporary place to prototype a project. You just plug them in and even plug the Arduino in to direct your project.

MaKey MaKey

If you are not ready for the whole Arduino experience, you could consider a MaKey MaKey. This device resulted from a very successful Kickstarter.com campaign in 2012. It is a card that has ports to attach devices, as well as a USB port that you cable back to a computer. Generally, any software that uses the computer keyboard and mouse can be controlled through the MaKey MaKey—well, not just by the MaKey MaKey but by whatever you connect to the ports on the device that control the keyboard and mouse. So, you can use alligator clips to connect a banana to the spacebar and touch the banana to use the spacebar. Or you can create a control panel for a game on a piece of paper, with controls drawn with pencil graphite that have alligator clips on them. Aside from existing software, there are programs created for the MaKey MaKey, and you can create your own with Scratch (an open-source programming tool discussed later). You have to keep the MaKey MaKey plugged into your computer to access the software and give the device power. Although it is something of a limited version of an Arduino, it can still teach patrons quite a bit about how devices (and even bananas) interact with software.

Raspberry Pi

The Raspberry Pi is similar to the first two devices in this section, but it takes things a step or two further. Not much larger than an Arduino (see figure 8.2), the Raspberry Pi is effectively a credit card–sized computer. You just need to plug in a television, a keyboard, an SD card for added memory, and a network cable to get it on the web. It will work fine as a computer for basic tasks, from making spreadsheets to playing video. You can also use its capacities as a microcontroller by adding programs into its built in memory. Generally, though, the projects that you might want to undertake with an Arduino are going to be a little more involved with the Raspberry Pi. It has greater capabilities than the Arduino and is a great next step for more complex projects. Sansing (2013) offers some excellent tips for starting off with Raspberry Pi in the library setting. One source to turn to for projects is the community at Element 14 (http://www.element14.com).

LEGO Mindstorms and LEGO WeDo

Now, another route to turn to with making things go is something that is focused on robotics. You can do robotics projects with the Arduino and the Raspberry Pi, but these LEGO products are dedicated to that outcome. They tend to be focused more on kids (WeDo for younger kids), but they are a lot of fun. There are many projects for each of these sets on the LEGO site, as well as on YouTube and elsewhere (see figure 8.3 for an

Figure 8.3. 40365 Line Follower Robot. *Image provided through a CC BY 2.0 License by chauro-mano, http://www.flickr.com/photos/chauromano/5627007458*

example). The kits have a lot of flexibility in what you can create with them, but they do guarantee a much more direct path to seeing a robot in action than some of the more free-form kits and items (Martinez and Stager 2013).

Making E-Textiles

An interesting tilt from the things-that-go and electronics categories are e-textiles, or adding circuitry and automation to fabrics. Two examples to have in mind are soft circuits and projects using the Lilypad, a variant of the Arduino. Soft circuits provide a way to create wearable electronics by adding circuits to clothing and other items. They range in complexity from something along the lines of sewing an LED throwie into your shirt to putting a microcontroller in a jacket to guide patterned lights and even music (Kemp 2013, 140). The idea is that anything you can do with circuits on a breadboard, you can sew into a garment and have it happen while you wear it. You use conductive thread to connect the components while also connecting the whole product to the fabric. The Lilypad is a microcontroller that is designed for work with textiles, and it offers the abil-ity to locate programming into the process. As figure 8.4 demonstrates, the Lilypad is a lilypad-shaped Arduino that can lie flat in a garment and control the lights and sounds and whatever else you add into the fabric. If you want a pattern to slowly appear on the sleeves of your shirt in neon green and red lights, you can make it happen. There are many exciting projects for both soft circuits and the Lilypad at Instructables.com.

Changing Things with Electronic Devices

A popular activity in makerspaces is to have programs in which patrons take appliances or other devices apart to see how they work and what else can be made with the parts. The

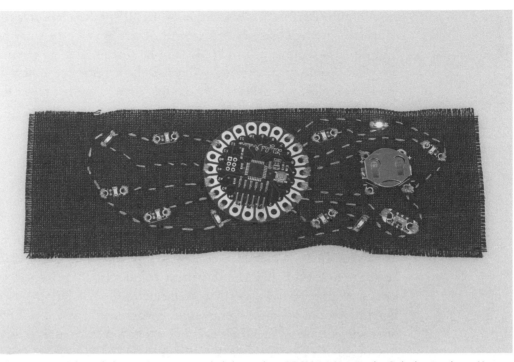

Figure 8.4. Lilypad demo. *Image provided through a CC BY 2.0 License by Solarbotics, http://www. flickr.com/photos/solarbotics/8695801961*

next step with this is to add something onto an existing product to make it do more. Toy hacking is one method for doing this: taking an existing toy and adding circuitry and/or microcontrollers to it to make it look or do something special. The following profile of the ideaLAB at the Denver Public Library mentions this activity. From footballs to dolls to radio-controlled cars, the sky is the limit. You can find many examples on Instructables. com. This is an application of the earlier technologies in this chapter to teach people to modify items and upgrade their capabilities.

Programming

In addition to being used for tasks in the prior category of making, programming can be an activity taught, learned, and practiced in the makerspace on its own merits. Programming can be used to create games, Internet applications, animations, and more. Scratch and Python are open-source programming languages that are often used in makerspaces. They both have educational uses and are relatively easy languages to learn. This makes them perfect for the makerspace environment. They also both have lots of examples, or libraries, available that can be used or modified as part of a new program. You can learn more about them and find suggested projects by visiting the Scratch (http://scratch.mit.edu/starter_projects/) and Python (http://www.python .org/about/apps/) sites.

Making Games and Apps

Another programming direction for makerspaces is to offer instruction and facilities for creating games and mobile apps. Games could be programmed using Scratch or Python for desktops and laptops, but mobile games could follow the same process as other mobile apps. Smith (2013) offers a selection of sites that offer platforms for creating apps, most of which have free versions to start with. These are all easy entry points to coding apps. You can also write apps in HTML and JavaScript. The big questions to start out with are what operating system you will create the app for and how you will distribute it. It is a great project for makers to try creating something that they can they download onto their phones and see in action.

Making Websites and Online Portfolios

Another direction to take programming instruction and practice in makerspaces is toward building websites. There are many venues for building an online presence, such as Facebook or Twitter or blogs, in which you can easily add text and images about yourself and what you are interested in. If you would like to have more flexibility in how you display information online, you can pursue building your own website. The programming language to learn is HTML (hypertext markup language). There are many free website locations out there to host your work, including Google Sites, Wix.com, and Weebly.com. Even if you are going to work within environments where you mostly do not need to program your own HTML, you will find that you can modify existing text by going into the source of a page and tweaking the code. HTML is a lot of fun to work with because everyone makes his or her code freely available for you to sample. There are countless sites that define HTML elements and give examples on how to use them. It is a great skill to teach your makers so that they can control how information about themselves and their projects is shared.

Making E-Books

Another natural area of interest for library makers is creating e-books. It is another form of creation that can utilize various software tools for creating documents, gathering and editing images, and then assembling them into an electronic book. Of particular note in this area is Apple's iBooks Author, which creates e-books that are then available for use on iPads and other iOS devices. Encheff (2013) describes the process that she used with a class of fifth graders to create an iBook. There are other products for creating e-books on additional platforms but none that are free with as wide a distribution opportunity (Stark 2012). Whether for group publishing project or individual efforts, giving your patrons the potential to self-produce a book can be a very appealing option.

◎ Electronics, Robotics, and Programming Shopping List

So what do you need (in addition to the products mentioned so far) to make these activities possible? Minimally, you'll need a computer of some kind (maybe just a Raspberry Pi, a television, and a memory card). Of course, having multiple people working on programming projects and uploading sketches to their Arduinos will require multiple computers. Perhaps you can make use of an existing computer lab in the library for instructing people in these projects. Arduino, Lilypad, MaKey MaKey, and Raspberry Pi projects will require the purchase of many small electrical components, such as resistors, light sensors, and other devices, as well as wire, conductive thread, and alligator clips. Much will depend on the precise project that you have in mind or how complete an array of options you would like to provide. For the most part, soldering will not be needed for these projects, but that is an option to add on for more involved or permanent circuit board or related constructions. Some basic hand tools (pliers, scissors, and screwdrivers) and sewing items would be helpful.

⊚ Refills Needed

Many materials needed for the activities are reusable. There will likely be needs to replace batteries, add tape for throwies, replace wires, and provide textiles and thread. Another replacement item might be new Arduinos or Lilypads as they are put into permanent use in products.

⊚ Special Space Requirements and Options

Space needs will depend on what you want to do. The work is not necessarily noisy or dangerous, though care must be taken with the electrical elements. Sufficient space is needed to spread out items during assembly of the electronic projects, as is easy access to computers for programming and e-book creation. Working with the electronic items will mean a lot of spare parts and gear to store, and if dedicated space is not available, then there will have to be somewhere to store things. One final thing to consider is the option of circulating Arduino, MaKey MaKey, and Raspberry Pi kits for patrons to use beyond the library (as done at the Johnson County Library, profiled next).

⊚ Library Makerspace Profile: Johnson County Library, Overland Park, KS

http://www.jocolibrary.org/makerspace

Meredith Nelson, Maker/Business Reference Librarian

How Did Your Makerspace Come to Be?

Nelson is the business reference librarian at her library (figure 8.5) and was advocating that changes be made to the library space to help provide resources for small businesses and people working from home. She wanted to add workshops on Adobe Creative Suite or other professional-grade software to increase the skills of these individuals. The topic of makerspaces was percolating in the library world, and she and her supervisor thought that they could combine a media lab with a makerspace. They did not start off with the idea of a makerspace for teens but rather came at this with a goal of exposing people to possibilities and giving them a space to practice higher-end computer skills. They saw a lot of overlap in bringing in high-tech items that could meet multiple objectives.

After the makerspace was equipped through an initial set of purchases, the library administration supported them in continuing to add technologies. They were able to keep up with patron requests while waiting for the addition of a 3D scanner in 2014. They have

Figure 8.5. Johnson County Library makerspace. *Image provided by Meredith Nelson*

been keeping up well, maintaining sufficient consumables for their 3D printer, and they have not had to charge patrons a fee for printing, although they are considering this due to increasing usage or perhaps adding a second 3D printer. Nelson notes that they are lucky to have a supportive administration that has responded to the busy nature of the space. It helps that the makerspace room has lots of windows and is very visible.

Who Uses It?

They have had regular use of the 3D printer, which was an exciting new concept for the library's patrons. There are always jobs in the queue, with a much wider range of uses than anticipated. Teens have printed props to use in school plays, for instance. There is also much interest in software, but no classes on using the various packages are in place yet. The library is setting up tutorials to give people chances to learn coding skills. There is a lot of interest in digital media but also in electronics. They offer soldering and Arduino kits as well as software, and soldering interest has decreased some over time. Their sewing machine is getting a lot of use. They offer a class in Scratch programming. There has also been a lot of interest in MaKey MaKeys, and they have added circulating Arduino kits in response to the demand. Nelson said that they are trying to make the space interactive enough, and one way that they do this is to require patron input before they buy new technologies. A recent addition was an EggBot.

How Do You Market the Makerspace?

Nelson and her colleagues started by offering an initial set of maker programs and spreading the word through various means. They offered "take it apart" days to build interest in the other offerings. The location of the makerspace provides a lot of marketing opportunities since it is right in the middle of the library. Many patrons ask questions about it and wander in. Another marketing tool is a weekly open house for the makerspace. It is a day on which no one can reserve the space and it is available. They set up demonstrations on that day and provide a time when patrons can come and see what is available and get some general questions answered. They have a full-page ad in the library's programming guide that is sent out to all of the library's locations. Nelson has also been talking to local maker groups and teachers and giving them tours so that their groups and classes can come out and get involved. She and her colleagues also had a booth at the local maker faire where they had a button maker in operation to connect with people who were interested in making.

Who Supports the Makerspace?

They have provided staff training to increase the number of people who can assist patrons. They have offered tours for library employees a couple of times per year, and the staff can earn their annual required educational credits by using the space. There is a growing team of staff members who can run the Makerbot. Beyond Nelson, just a few people know how to use Adobe Illustrator, Final Cut Pro, and some of the other software. There is a collection of reference books that stays in the makerspace room. They also have some Lynda.com videos available to help with questions, and they are adding a subscription to Treehouse.com. Unfortunately, there is not much one-on-one support available, but they are trying to build ways to connect people with support. Nelson's duties are split between the makerspace and her business responsibilities.

How Do You Stay Aware of Developments in Makerspaces?

Nelson is grateful that so many makerspaces have shared their programming ideas; the "take it apart" program is a one example. She turned to Chicago's Innovation Lab for ideas on programming to run with the 3D printer. This taught her to show people the process of using it and then give them examples of products to print. When the makerspace started, there were few options to turn to, but now there are examples all over the place. She has borrowed ideas from others and hopes that they will borrow from her in return.

What Do You See Happening in Your Makerspace in the Next Year?

The library's youth services team is interested in making, and Nelson is creating maker kits that can go out to the library's 13 locations with them to use for programs. They plan to add another sewing machine and an embroidery machine. Nelson has encouraged the youth services group to use the electronics kits, but the group is a bit intimidated by them at the moment. There is a huge interest in creating video kits with laptops, cameras, and microphones and then offering programs on using them to make videos. The central location will be undergoing a renovation in the next year or two, and Nelson is trying to get a sound or video booth added at that point.

What Is Your Advice to Others Who Would Like to Create a Makerspace?

You do not need a room or a space. You can just start with LEGOs or LED throwies and get kids involved. Just put out a set of littleBits in the children's room and see what happens. Nelson always encourages librarians to put up a whiteboard, ask people what

Figure 8.6. ideaLAB. *Image provided by Nate Stone*

they want, and then build from their suggestions. If people suggested knitting needles, she would buy them and see if they get used. Connect with other people, and if they are interested, see what they can offer in terms of ideas or volunteer time. Everyone has something to offer and something to teach. Just be open to ideas.

Library Makerspace Profile: ideaLAB, Denver Public Library, Denver, CO

http://teens.denverlibrary.org/idealab

Nate Stone, Library Program Associate

How Did Your Makerspace Come to Be?

The Community Technology Center at the Denver Public Library has offered technology instruction since 2008, from moving a mouse to learning basic CSS programming. But it was looking for opportunities to expand its offerings, specifically moving into media creation, and it decided to seek funding for a teen lab. It found an opportunity for a grant through the Colorado Library Service and Technology Act and received an initial $20,000. It then found a vacant room to use and created ideaLAB in May 2013 (figure 8.6). Even before the grant, the center started a teen tech club and hung out in one of the computer classrooms, using open-source software to do game design and photo editing. Soon it had a devoted group of teens who were interested in what it was doing. Stone was greatly inspired by the example of YouMedia in Chicago and the Intel Computer Clubhouse Network. Both work with kids to use technology and art and to become life-long learners.

The Denver Public Library heavily supports ideaLAB. It is in the process of having the lab move from a 480-square-foot room to a new 1,000-square-foot room. There is an ongoing commitment by the library to pay for staffing, and now Stone and his colleagues are experimenting with raising funds for additional equipment. They asked teens to suggest what they felt was missing from the makerspace. They then launched an Indiegogo campaign to fund as much as they could from the list of "missing stuff." The campaign was a moderate success, with about $5,000 raised of the $7,500 worth of equipment the teens asked for. A lot of community partners are really excited about the teen tech lab and have been giving them stuff. They held a "build your own computer" program, and a group gave them computer parts for free. They have received great training opportunities from SparkFun (http://www.sparkfun.com) and have received free equipment from it, such as Arduinos.

Who Uses It?

Right now, only teens 12 to 19 years old are allowed in the space, and they are predominantly boys around 14. They come from throughout the Denver metro area and are primarily interested in shooting video. The teens are making movies and using various digital technologies, including Photoshop and tablets for drawing. The music studio also sees a lot of use, and the lab has an active community of Minecraft players and modders.

How Do You Market the Makerspace?

The center started with a marketing blitz of local schools that included every middle school and high school in a three-mile radius from the central library. It sent out flyers and contacted technology teachers and librarians in schools. Stone and his colleagues then had the opportunity for an appearance on a morning show and an article in the local paper.

The majority of hours in the ideaLAB are "open lab" time, where teens can work on whatever they want. At the beginning, they decided to engage teens with a formal class one night per week (e.g., Adobe Illustrator). The response from teens was not positive: they had just been in school and did not want to sit through another class. Instead, Stone and colleagues switched their focus to more informal programming: project cards that teens can work on when they are interested in trying something out, working on sample projects during lab time to spark teens' interests, and making any formal programs project based. They have also added programming to fit teen interests, such as Minecraft parties and toy hacking, and then ones that feature more career-oriented information. They have tried to connect teens with people who do the same stuff outside the library walls but are paid for it. They had some independent game designers come in and talk to the teens about how they learned to do their work. The main lesson that they learned was that teens generally respond better to programming that is as little like school as possible: providing more informal ways to learn, based on their own interests and focused on discrete manageable projects, was far more successful.

The goal for the grant proposal was that the lab would reach 50 individual kids over the course of 100 visits in the first year. Instead, it had a total of 150 individuals and 400 visits in the first 4 months and so felt swamped and stopped outreach for a time.

Who Supports It?

There are five staff members from the library's Community Technology Center who work in the lab. It is open 20 hours a week, and most of that is open lab time. There is always staff on hand to help the teens out, supplemented by 10 or 11 volunteers who provide assistance. In addition, a local art institute has college students studying graphic design who are on work study helping out in the ideaLAB.

How Do You Stay Aware of Developments in Makerspaces?

Stone and his colleagues toured a bunch of hackerspaces and makerspaces in Denver to get ideas: Denhac (http://denhac.org), the Concoctory (http://concoctory.com), and a bunch of local libraries with makerspaces to see what they do to structure their spaces. This really helped them visualize some options that are going into their new space planning. The main thing that they learned was to be as flexible as possible.

Programming ideas come from the people who use the space, and the teens have made lots of suggestions. Minecraft has been an attraction. They worked with the teens to create a stomp pad with a MaKey MaKey to control a character, and then they built a giant axe that one could use to mine things. They have also been working with community partners who have fantastic ideas. Sparkfun does microcontroller programs in schools and elsewhere, and it has been willing to share its curriculum with the library. Some members of the library staff who are not directly involved in ideaLAB have become known as experts. For instance, a staff member who records music at home but never mentioned it at work has become a resource for the music studio.

Stone and his colleagues learn a lot by just doing what they think is cool. They spent over a year and a bunch of money interviewing people and talking to the community to come up with ideas for the space. But the truth of the *Field of Dreams* saying has been shown to them: "If you build it, they will come." They can always find people who are interested in what they want to try. A lot of their development is driven by what staff want to do; they have taken their passion and used that to build the same passion with the teens. This models and, hopefully, inspires lifelong learning among those who experience the makerspace.

What Do You See Happening in Your Makerspace in the Next Year?

In 2014, they are expanding their offerings to include adult and family programming, and they are figuring out how to reach out to these groups. Part of their space is a music studio, and adults have asked if they could use it during off-hours. They were not able to offer those hours and did receive some complaints from adults. With their new space, they can handle activities across multiple ages.

What Is Your Advice to Others Who Would Like to Create a Makerspace?

The focus should be on getting the most bang for your buck. Libraries have to find the sweet spot. Some technology is not very expensive, and just about anyone can buy it on one's own, but some technology is way beyond the library's budget. So the library has to pursue stuff that is just out of reach for individuals but still affordable for the library. We are creating collective resources to give people access to specialized tools. It is similar to how libraries buy lots of books and not all of them get used.

Stone would have started community outreach even earlier than he did. He could have brought in more experts ahead of time and then had them share their knowledge in the library. That would have saved him and his staff time from learning how to do it on their own.

His unit provides technology training for both the public and the library staff. Some staff members are terrified of the maker technology, and he and his colleagues have been trying to impart to them that this technology is not different from anything else they are using. If they do not know something, they need to use their skills to find the answer, without being scared.

You do not need a lot of money. Something useful will get going with just a few easy purchases: a decent Mac, a microphone, and a keyboard. Arapahoe Public Library turned a closet into a little lab to edit video and music and now has people coming in and recording songs—all for $2,000. There is a lot of open-source software available that can help libraries cut costs when building makerspaces, programs such as the GIMP or Inkscape.

⑨ Key Points

Electronics, robotics, and programming activities can serve a variety of purposes in a library makerspace.

- Patrons can learn the basics of how electrical devices work and how to create simple examples of them.
- Microcontrollers allow for more advanced projects that operate under programmed routines.
- Programming can be taught as a stand-alone activity or used in tandem with other creative activities.

Turn to chapter 9 for a discussion of how items designed in software can be formed into physical objects through 3D printing.

⑨ References

Encheff, Dana. 2013. "Creating a Science E-Book with Fifth Grade Students." *Techtrends: Linking Research & Practice to Improve Learning* 57 (6): 61–72.

Hammond, Keith. 2013. "Extreme LED Throwies." *Makezine* (blog). http://makezine.com/projects/extreme-led-throwies/.

Kemp, Adam. 2013. *The Makerspace Workbench: Tools, Technologies, and Techniques for Making*. Sebastopol, CA: Maker Media.

Martinez, Sylvia Libow, and Gary Stager. 2013. *Invent to Learn: Making, Tinkering, and Engineering in the Classroom*. Torrance, CA: Constructing Modern Knowledge Press.

Melgar, Enrique Ramos, and Ciriaco Castro Diez. 2012. *Arduino and Kinect Projects: Design, Build, and Blow Their Minds*. New York: Apress.

O'Neill, Terence, and Josh Williams. 2014. *Arduino*. Ann Arbor, MI: Cherry Lake.

Sansing, Chad. 2013. "Life with Raspberry Pi: Sparking a School Coding Revolution." *Digital Shift* (blog). August 19. http://www.thedigitalshift.com/2013/08/k-12/life-with-raspberry-pi-this-slim-25-computer-is-hot-and-showing-no-signs-of-cooling-off-it-may-just-spark-a-coding-revolution-in-schools/.

Smith, Grace. 2013. "Ten Excellent Platforms for Building Mobile Apps." *Mashable* (blog). December 3. http://mashable.com/2013/12/03/build-mobile-apps/.

Stark, Chelsea. 2012. "How iBooks Author Stacks Up to the Competition." *Mashable* (blog). January 23. http://mashable.com/2012/01/23/ibooks-author-self-publishing-comparison/

Thomas, AnnMarie. 2013. "Squishy Circuits." In *Design, Make, Play: Growing the Next Generation of STEM Innovators*, edited by Margaret Honey and David Kanter, 119–37. New York: Routledge.

CHAPTER 9

Resources for
3D Printing and Prototyping

3D PRINTING IS THE SIGNATURE ELEMENT OF MAKERSPACES, providing iconic images and video of the creation of three-dimensional items from colorful plastic. Although by now it should be clear that makerspaces include all kinds of making, 3D printing is more than just a mascot. There are intriguing possibilities attached to the process of fabricating objects on your desktop rather than in a factory. Since the first inexpensive 3D printer was produced in 2007, models have been progressively

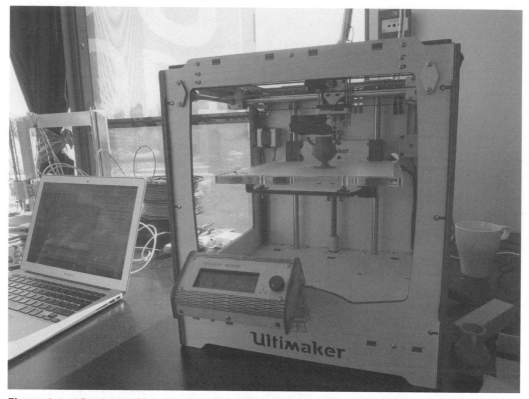

Figure 9.1. 3D printer Ultimaker. *Image provided through a CC BY 2.0 License by Mirko Tobias Schaefer (Gastev), http://www.flickr.com/photos/gastev/9319065887*

modified by the open-source community to keep lowering the price and widen the reach of these devices (Kemp 2013). At its simplest end, 3D printing is about small plastic items that may meet practical needs and allow larger creations to be prototyped. At its most futuristic extent, this method of creation is imagined to be able to form just about anything, right in the privacy of your home. Nearer to this future are amazing items being made today, such as 3D-printed human hips and artificial heart valves. It is a rapidly progressing technology with a range of creations that are hard to bookend. See figure 9.1 for an example.

The informal survey of library makerspaces (see the appendix for details) revealed that 50 of the 109 respondents (46 percent) offer 3D printing. In addition, 34 (31 percent) offer 3D modeling, most likely with software such as SketchUp or CAD (computer-aided design). A final relevant category from the survey was prototyping, offered by 21 respondents (19 percent). Prototyping is defined as creating models of a product or solution that you hope to create but need to test first, and it can be done in ways other than 3D printing. Likewise, 3D printers are used for much more than prototyping. This chapter is likely the best place to make note of prototyping, since it is something that can be pursued in a makerspace and certainly done with 3D printing. Overall, 3D printing is widely available in library makerspaces (Gallant 2013) and is likely to grow given the developments detailed here.

◎ What Your Patrons Could Be Making

Aside from the short list of objects mentioned so far, patrons of your library makerspace could make all sorts of things. Just picking at random from a page of results on the Yeggi.

com design search engine, they could make an iPhone stand, a castle, a clock, a stamp, a safety razor, a BB-gun pellet trap, a wrench, a whistle, an aquaponics grow bed, a padlock with key, and on and on (see figure 9.2 for one example). None of these products might interest you, but you can always make something that you would be interested in. It might be more useful, though, to talk about the different directions that patrons' 3D making could take. Think of these as categories of making that they could pursue. More of the how-to and design sources for 3D printing follow.

Prototyping

Makers could turn to the 3D printer with prototyping in mind. They could use the tools of 3D printing to create a model of a desired end product. They might be making it at a smaller size or of a different type of material than the end product—and the final item may not be created with a 3D printer at all. The idea behind prototyping is to test a concept out before you take the time to create something that might be more time-consuming or expensive to make. The 3D printer does the making for you, layer after layer, all for the cost of a little plastic.

Final Product

Alternatively, maybe the object created *is* the final product. It could be a stand-alone item that serves a purpose all by itself. It could be a solid piece, or it could contain moving parts. It could be a part of another whole item or maybe a missing piece. If you have ever broken a piece off of something, lost a game piece, or just needed one more of those clips to get the shower curtain hanging right, you could print it out. Patrons could walk away with the completion of an existing item or a new beginning with something that stands alone.

Figure 9.2. *Make:* magazine 3D printer shootout. *Image provided through a CC BY 2.0 License by John Abella (jabella), http://www.flickr.com/photos/jabella/9440443380*

Self-Designed Objects

3D print jobs can be printed from designs from a patron's own head . . . well, not directly, but through the mechanism of 3D design software (discussed in detail in the next section). An imagined item can be brought into digital existence on a computer and then transmitted into three-dimensionality with the 3D printer.

Other-Designed Objects

The printed 3D objects can also be items designed by someone else. This can be a very satisfying and relatively easy project for someone new to 3D printing: find a 3D item online and then print it out. It is a magical experience to hold something that you have previously seen only on the screen.

Crowdsourced Objects

As a cross between the prior two options, your patron might show her or his own talents by modifying an already existing design. This collaboration between a person in the flesh and one or more digital creators of an object leads to a final object that owes its existence to multiple authors. To further extend the path of this object, your patron might share the design online, where a larger crowd might continue its development.

⊚ How Does 3D Printing Work?

3D printers create objects by applying multiple layers of material to a surface. This process is known as *additive layer manufacturing*, in which successive layers of material are extruded out of the printer head to complete a design (O'Neill and Williams 2014). 3D objects are thus built from the ground up; the item that you are printing grows taller as the material piles up. You can watch the printer lay down material in one area of your creation and then skip over others to allow for curves, holes, or markings in the item. The printer follows along its path, completing the needed material or skipping the laying down of the material in each zone of the object, until the design is complete and it can rest. This can be seen in part in figure 9.3.

The 3D printers that you will see in a library makerspace use plastic as their medium. The plastic filament, which can be any color or clear, needs to be melted by the printer to create the image. Picture it like a colorful piece of spaghetti, wound around a spool for storage, from which it is fed into the printer. It is possible to use multiple colors in 3D printing by changing out the filament partway into the job but not to have colors alternate across each layer. You can make a statue that is red at the bottom and yellow on top. The plastic object can also be painted to allow for a more colorful result.

The plastic comes in two varieties: first, ABS (acrylonitrile butadiene styrene), which tends to make a sturdier object, as befits the material that is used for LEGO bricks; second, PLA (polylactide), which tends to be cheaper than ABS and is also more flexible (Martinez and Stager 2013). Depending on your 3D printer, you might be able to use both types, with different heat settings in place for each. And the medium for printing is not limited to plastic, either. There are industrial and specialty 3D printers that print objects with metal, ceramics, glass, and concrete. Consumer 3D printers are just starting to have the capacity to print metallic objects (Lipson and Kurman 2013).

Figure 9.3. Probibliot31. *Image provided through a CC BY 2.0 License by FryskLab, http://www.flickr. com/photos/83026924@N03/12464584064*

3D printing is varied and plastic, but it is not a fast process. Depending on the size of the object and the thickness of the plastic, the whole process can take anywhere from a few hours to a few days. This definitely influences expectations on being able to quickly produce items with this technology. Videos of 3D printers at work are exciting to watch, but you have to keep in mind that they generally compress time by quite a bit. It is crucial when planning workshops on 3D design and printing to remember that the participants will not be able to walk away with a finished product at the end of the hour. Library makerspaces with 3D printers have to set up processes for providing users with estimates on when printing jobs will complete, as suggested in the profile of the Hunt Library at North Carolina State University later in this chapter.

Why Do Makers Want to Use 3D Printing?

Aside from the wow factor of 3D printing, what draws people to use it? What keeps people working on new printers and techniques? Lipson and Kurman (2013) offer a list of 10 appealing aspects of 3D printing today and in the near future. The following are the seven that are most representative of current printing capacities in the library makerspace:

- More complex designs do not cost more to print than simple designs.
- The printer can make multiple shapes and designs without having to change the equipment in any way.
- 3D objects can be printed with moving parts all at once, in the same design.
- The printer allows for intricate designs that are impossible for traditional machinery and methods.
- The main skill required for printing is to be able to create the design file rather than run the equipment.

- Consumer 3D printers have a very small footprint but can still make fairly large objects.
- It is possible to scan physical items and reproduce them exactly with the 3D printer.

The appeal of fashioning something out of nothing but an idea in your head is constant across different media of construction. There is something different in 3D printing, though, which combines the relatively low investments of skill and human effort with a very flexible piece of equipment to produce an extremely well-detailed outcome. You could argue from that line of thought that humans are inherently lazy and will also choose the flashiest option over ones of better quality. Furthermore, not all parts of the 3D-printing process are simple to enact or are without room for failure in the design, the medium, or the equipment. With these questions in mind, what appears true about 3D printing is that as the equipment grows cheaper and more widely available, there is no shortage of makers continuing to join in and push the boundaries of this mode of creation.

◎ Tools for 3D Creation

3D printing makes it possible to imagine an object, design it on a computer, and then bring it into being. To do this, all that you need is a design file and a 3D printer. There are many choices of printers and methods for obtaining a design, however. This section of the chapter examines options among printers, sources for existing designs, software to use in creating new designs, and methods for scanning 3D objects.

3D Printers

For library makerspaces, 3D printers will tend to be consumer-oriented devices in the range of $4,000 or less. They all use a process known as FDM (fused deposition modeling) to create items, which involves the melting of plastic and the process of spreading layers described earlier. A useful list of printers and their characteristics is found in "3D Printer Comparison" (2014), including current prices for the equipment. One sample printer is shown in figure 9.4. The printers come with software to transmit the 3D design file to the printer. As with many products, you tend to get what you pay for, with increased features or speed available in the more expensive models. Here are short synopses of three printers, which point out some of the choices that you have when selecting one.

Makerbot Replicator 2

Makerbot is a very popular brand of 3D printers, with its devices featured in many of the makerspace profiles in this book and in the literature on library makerspaces. The Replicator 2 (see https://store.makerbot.com/replicator2 for more information) prints using PLA filament and costs around $2,200. It offers a larger maximum size for a printed object (11.2 × 6 × 6.1 in.) than the other two listed here. It is also a bit faster, depending on the object to be printed. Makerbot has been in the business for a long time and has a large community of users to draw on. It also created Thingiverse.com, a huge collection of 3D design files that can be printed on the Makerbot. So the Replicator 2 prints larger objects with lots of community support fairly quickly but is more expensive than the other two. If you would like the flexibility of larger items, it might be worth paying more up front.

Figure 9.4. Makerbot Industries, Replicator 2, 3D printer 15. *Image provided through a CC BY 2.0 License by Creative Tools, http://www.flickr.com/photos/creative_tools/8080033501*

Afinia H-Series

Afinia's printer uses both PLA and ABS and is sold at $1,600. The H-Series (see http://www.afinia.com/3d-printers) print objects at a little over 5 cubic inches (5.5 × 5.5 × 5.3) and is slower than the Replicator 2. However, it does have a lower cost and offers greater flexibility in taking both kinds of plastics. It is supposed to have a more plug-and-play setup experience. With the Afinia, you pay less for the printer and get a possibly easier setup, but the items that you print are smaller than what is possible on the Replicator 2. The trade-off of cost and object size might make sense if your intended printing is not going to grow beyond the maximum item size.

RepRap Mendel

Could you save money by building your own 3D printer? Yes, indeed! The RepRap project (http://reprap.org/wiki) offers free plans for creating a 3D printer for $600 or less. There are multiple models to choose from, with Mendel being the latest one. The Mendel (see http://reprap.org/wiki/Mendel) prints both PLA and ABS filament. It prints objects up to 8 × 8 × 5.5 in.—so a bit larger than the Afinia and a bit smaller than the Replicator 2. The speed of printing is closer to the Afinia than to the Replicator 2. For this printer, you can pay less and get a larger maximum size item than the Afinia, while continuing to have flexibility in plastics. It is much cheaper than the Replicator 2 and only slightly smaller in maximum size. The real question comes in your willingness to make a RepRap Mendel by yourself.

An interesting aspect of the project is that it is aimed toward making a self-replicating device so that many of the parts of the printer can be printed by another RepRap printer. So, you could reach out to a member of the RepRap community and see if someone would be willing to assist you in this process. As the wiki recommends, you have to be interested in not only 3D printing but also the journey of making such a printer.

3D Design Collections

When you are looking for something to print on your 3D printer, note that there is a growing collection of 3D designs available for anyone to access and print as is or to modify per your own wishes. Thingiverse.com has been around the longest and is the largest current collection. The RepRap Object Library (http://reprap.org/wiki/The_RepRap_Object_Library) has a small selection to draw from. YouMagine.com and Cubehero.com are relatively new additions as spots to share and locate designs. In attempting to make searching across these collections and other smaller ones easier, Bld3r.com shows results from all the object repositories from its site and serves as a place to upload your designs, while Yeggi.com serves as a search engine of all the sites. The idea here is that there are many places to see if someone has already invented the wheel that you were about to unknowingly reinvent and many places to be inspired to create or modify your own version for printing.

3D Design Software

If you cannot find an existing design for an object or you need to modify one, you will need to turn to 3D design software. There are three great ones to use, all of which have a free version. SketchUp (http://www.sketchup.com) has a Make version for free and a Pro version for purchase. It is available for both Windows and Mac. Blender (http://www.blender.org) is an open-source tool that meets a variety of 3D modeling needs in addition to 3D printing. It is available for download for Windows, Mac, and Linux. Finally, Autodesk 123D (http://www.123dapp.com) offers a number of apps that can be downloaded for Windows or Mac or used as web-based apps. Two merit special mention here: 123D Design is a free tool for 3D creation and editing similar to SketchUp and Blender, and 123D Catch can transform photographs and other digital images into 3D design files. Figure 9.5 has an example of a 3D-modeled item being created in Blender.

3D Scanning

Another route to take toward creating a needed 3D design file is to use a 3D scanner or a related method. In fact, the 123D Catch app is a method of 3D scanning in that you can take a picture of an object or a person and have the app create a 3D file. You could also use a MakerBot Digitizer desktop 3D scanner (http://store.makerbot.com/digitizer), which can scan an object up to 8 in. across and 8 in. tall. There is also the ability to use an Xbox-360 Kinect for 3D scanning (a game controller that you operate by having it continuously scan your body); directions for doing so are available at http://www.instructables.com/id/EASY-Kinect-3D-Scanner/. Patrons check the Kinect out for this purpose at Hunt Library at North Carolina State University (profiled later in this chapter).

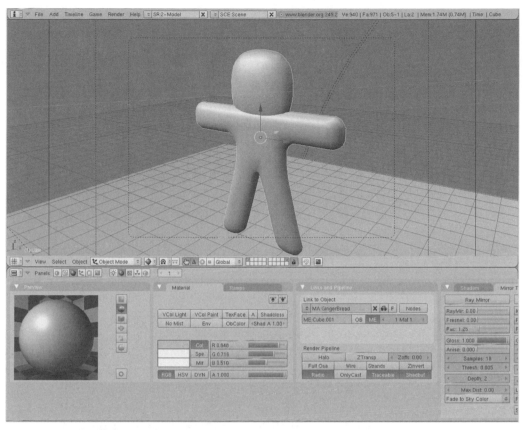

Figure 9.5. Blender tutorial 3. *Image provided through a CC BY 2.0 License by 4everMiku, http://www.flickr.com/photos/4evermiku/5036052148*

⑥ Refills Needed

The main replacement needed for 3D printing is plastic. Many 3D printers come with a starter amount of filament, and it is helpful to note how quickly you use the filament for early testing and projects so that you can plan ahead and stock up. Other ongoing costs will be there for print maintenance and repair. The printer needs to be oiled on occasion, and it may wear out some of its parts (for which you could potentially print replacements using the printer, assuming that a key part is not broken). Repairs of the printers are generally not difficult, but they do require the person making the repairs to be brave enough to open the equipment up and make needed adjustments.

⑥ Special Space Requirements and Options

The small footprint of 3D printers and scanners means that not much space is needed for operating them. However, you will want to provide enough room to work with items that you are scanning or to open up the printer to clean it out or make adjustments. You will also need space for a computer that will transmit the 3D design to the printer and control the printing. A very key element for 3D printers is ventilation, which could be provided by locating the printer near a window or adding a local ventilation system (Kemp 2013). The printing process is not particular messy, but facets of finishing a 3D printed object can be. Sometimes, there are extra pieces of plastic called *supports* that print while connected to the object to scaffold it and keep it from falling as the object prints. The supports are broken off or otherwise removed once the job completes; the object is then sanded to remove any remaining support material.

Two last space-related issues are important to consider. One is providing enough space in the makerspace or the library to store the plastic that you will use. The other is to think ahead from your first 3D printer and about where you might put the second, third, fourth, or fifth printers if you build your service. You may find yourself wishing that you could follow the lead of FryskLab (profiled later in this chapter), which has 3D printers installed on the bus that makes up its mobile fab lab. That example shows that even minimal space can work.

⊚ Intellectual Property Considerations

Given that this technology allows you to create 3D objects of anything that you can scan or design, it is important to guide makers in questions of intellectual property. This is a topic that all makerspaces should cover, but library makerspaces are very well situated to talk about intellectual property concerns. Your library's mission typically contains a role or responsibility to be aware and give guidance in copyright and fair use provisions and questions. With the open-source collections of designs, the resulting objects can be printed without concern, as the designs are generally shared under Creative Commons licensing. However, if a patron wants to scan a trademarked action figure or design something that looks an awful lot like the logo of a sports team, caution is needed. If you are making something for your personal use, it might be fine, but selling a copy of an existing product or posting your design in an online collaborative could provoke a lawsuit (Martinez and Stager 2013). The role of library staff in a makerspace is to help makers build their understanding of these situations and navigate them as they arise.

⊚ The Future of 3D Printing

In both industrial and consumer applications, 3D printing is expected to grow and see further development of equipment and software. Printing with metal and other substances is expected to become widely available at a much lower cost with the addition of SLS (selective laser sintering) printers to the consumer market ("The Maker Movement" 2013). SLS printing exists in now very expensive 3D printers, but as the patents for SLS technology expire in 2014, less expensive printers should become available. A similar move occurred when patents for FDM 3D printers expired, leading to the current great growth in inexpensive FDM printers. Metal and plastic objects cover a great deal of products that people might decide to print on their own rather than purchase elsewhere. It could be that you will see very inexpensive (under $100) FDM 3D printers become available (Anderson 2012). Combination devices are already appearing that combine 3D printing and scanning with a computer numerical control router. There will be a very interesting time ahead for making physical items. For the moment, there are still questions of usefulness and cost issues that will keep 3D printing from the home market and a useful shared item for makerspaces (Gilpin 2014).

⊚ Library Makerspace Profile: Hunt Library, North Carolina State University Libraries, Raleigh, NC

http://www.lib.ncsu.edu/spaces/makerspace

Adam Rogers, Emerging Technology Services Librarian

How Did Your Makerspace Come to Be?

The inspiration for the space came from attending the 2012 Digital Media and Learning Conference put on by the MacArthur Foundation, which covered working on education, making, and tinkering. *Make:* magazine was there, and John Seely Brown spoke. The focus was not on academic libraries but on the makerspaces that were great examples to learn from. Rogers is a hobbyist and DIY (do-it-yourself) person, and he brings this outside interest into his work. The North Carolina State University libraries are very technology focused, with technology-lending programs and a sandbox project that put new technologies into the hands of students. There is a focus on exposing students to new ways of doing things. When iPads first came out, the library had them on hand to check out. Students started blogging about them and got the word out quickly. So the makerspace started in a setting with a focus on technology.

Hunt Library is the larger environment for the makerspace. It opened in 2013 on the university's Centennial Campus. The makerspace was a late addition to the Hunt Library plan, but it was able to find space in the new building. There were others in the library who thought a makerspace would be a great fit for the library, the campus, and the new building. They looked at the Delmar Library at the University of Nevada at Reno as a makerspace model; the Georgia Tech Invention Studio was also a model, although it is run by students and is not part of the library. All told, the team did lots of scanning around and then decided on equipment and gathering the tools that it needed to have in place. All of this could be done before it actually had the space together, while the library was being constructed. Since the Hunt Library would be on a new campus, the team had to consider what tools would work there. The library administration was very positive. Once team members had figured out the equipment that they had purchased, they then had to form policies to govern access to the tools.

It is a fairly small physical space. There is not enough room for students to work on projects in the space. The team would like to have more of a lab arrangement in which people could work independently. Right now, people come in and interact with staff, and the majority of those interactions involve talking to people, showing them how the machines work, and answering questions. This does lead to the provision of information literacy on the makerspace technology and informing students about such issues as intellectual property and 3D design software. The team gets many questions about what types of projects the machines are used for and what it costs to buy them and keep them running. This is an underreported role for library makerspaces: teaching people about technology that is new to them. From those interactions, the team gets people who decide that they want to use the machines, and many cool projects have come from people stumbling into the space on a library tour and then coming back.

Rogers thinks that there would be advantages to giving users direct access to the machines so that they can learn their limitations and how to fix them. He feels that they are missing out on learning by doing. But, on the positive side, the library is protected from dealing with these issues. This means that the library can help a larger number of people get access to the equipment and print things out without a lot of expertise. At this point, it is just not possible to leave the machines out for individuals to use. The team has had trouble figuring out service costs and open hours for such a service, which is separate from the rest of the library in terms of hours and in that it is very much hands-on for staff.

In terms of the financial end of the makerspace, the team had a budget for equipment but still needed to recover costs for resources. It has charged to recover some staff and machine costs over time. The makerspace has had such a positive response from the campus and the library administration. It has been awarded a grant from a university foundation for a new makerspace in the D. H. Hill Library, and there has been interest from alumni in supporting the current space.

Who Uses It?

Hunt Library is located on the Centennial Campus of North Carolina State, where the university's College of Engineering and College of Textiles are located. Many of those who use the makerspace are engineering students who have already learned 3D design as part of their courses. In another situation, it might have to provide more workshops on 3D design, but that is already happening in the classroom. It has primarily worked with undergraduates and graduate students but not very many faculty members yet. The team has also had some students from other disciplines come over from the university's North Campus.

There are other 3D printers on campus, but all are limited to users within a particular discipline. For instance, the College of Design has 3D printers of its own, and it subsidizes prices for print jobs for its students. The library makerspace has interacted with that college to share knowledge and to refer people to it for assistance. It is important that the library can serve as a place that provides access to this equipment for all departments and units.

Maker devices also fit in very well with the library's technology-lending program. It has added such makerspace items as Arduino kits, Raspberry Pi kits, MaKey MaKeys, and 3D scanners to the lending collection. The 3D scanner goes out for a 3-day loan. The team is trying to find a good balance between giving people enough time to complete a project and providing multiple people access to the items.

How Do You Market the Makerspace?

The main marketing method has been through library tours. The space has a prominent display of sample 3D items and a Makerbot on the main floor of library, which inspires new makers. The amount of foot traffic through the new library has helped, as has the potential for a large user base, given the engineering and design focus on the campus. It has seen a ton of use already and continually needs to focus on logistics and policies just to keep up. Rogers and his colleagues have done some open workshops on 3D printing and design to create interest. For these, they posted flyers and digital signage in the library. The team gives demonstrations of its equipment in freshman orientation sessions. It would also like to work with faculty on including making as part of their curriculum, but it does not have the space to accommodate a whole class in the makerspace.

Who Supports It?

The makerspace is primarily staffed by student workers under Rogers's direction. Their role is to assist users in the 3D printing service, part of which includes managing expectations of what users can get out of the machines. They show users examples of printed models and let them know how long jobs will take to print. The 3D printers are pretty straightforward to explain to people, and it is generally easy to go from a student presenting a file to getting that file set up in the queue to print. The laser cutter, however, takes more work to figure out. There are many more parameters to set, depending on whether you are cutting through an item or engraving on it, and so it takes a lengthier appointment to work through a conversation with a user.

What Do You See Happening in Your Makerspace in the Next Year?

North Carolina State University's libraries will open a second, larger makerspace in the D. H. Hill Library on its North Campus next year. They will need to do more outreach and teach more workshops to get this one rolling. They are having an internal debate on the future for both spaces, which essentially comes down to meeting two different needs at once. The Hunt Library makerspace has a demonstrated need for more higher-end 3D printers. It will move to partner more with others on campus to reduce any duplication of efforts, and it will seek to provide a more professional 3D printing service. At the same time, in the D. H. Hill space, the focus will be on creating an interdisciplinary DIY space for beginning users, getting new groups involved, and reaching students individually and through course projects. The hope is to be able to further define and succeed in these two service areas.

In both makerspaces, the library would like to improve the effectiveness of its 3D scanning by adding new scanners that that are more user-friendly. It would also like to increase the overall number of scanners that it has available. It would like to open up access to the laser cutter, which seems feasible given the greater amount of room in the new space. There will be moves to work with faculty to include Arduino and Raspberry Pi in course assignments and to teach some workshops on using them. Again, given the size of the new space, the library intends to hold more invents there and have it be a much more open environment that students and faculty can drop into. This will help the team build community within the makerspaces.

What Is Your Advice to Others Who Would Like to Create a Makerspace?

Think about access and cost issues and the user experience first rather than the machines themselves. Also, think about how users will learn to use the machines and how to scaffold their learning experiences. You need to think through how someone will actually move through the process of getting something printed in 3D. This involves everything from training staff so that everything moves smoothly to assessing how multiple print jobs will be queued and how you can give users estimates. It is so important to be able to communicate with users. It is possible to just set machines off to the side with a gatekeeper, but one has to think about how people can use them in a sustainable way.

Start small and have a system in place to gather feedback. Learn to tell the story of how the makerspace is being used so that you can add more users and gain support. Explain how people are using them to get things done.

ⓖ Library Makerspace Profile: Bibliotheekservice Fryslan (Friesland Library Service), Leeuwarden, Friesland, Netherlands

http://www.frysklab.nl

Jeroen de Boer, Domain Specialist for New Media

How Did Your Makerspace Come to Be?

De Boer started looking around and saw a growing connection between libraries and makerspaces in the United States, and about a year ago, he suggested starting a library makerspace in the Netherlands. This suggestion received a good response from his colleagues, and he started looking around his local community to find people who might be interested in starting a fab lab. He chose to pursue making a fab lab to connect with the large worldwide community connected to the fab lab movement. He held meetings in November 2012 and February 2013 to gather potential stakeholders and to discuss the initial plans. A key partner was the local makerspace in Leeuwarden.

At the February meeting, the group put on a hands-on maker session with a local school to give people an idea of what the fab lab might look like. It brought MaKey MaKeys and soldering kits to the school and started 80 students working on projects. The stakeholders entered the room and saw the students working and enjoying themselves, which convinced them to join the project. This enabled de Boer to move ahead and start planning a grant proposal. He first turned to contacts at other Dutch fab labs to help plan his group's approach. They were successful in achieving an official fab lab and became the first library in Europe to earn that designation.

The special aspect of the FryskLab (the name of the fab lab) is that it is completely mobile. The fab lab is located in a library bus and can be moved around to schools (figures 9.6 and 9.7). Mobility was deemed important to the project because of the library's location in a rural part of the Netherlands. It needed to be able to reach out to the area beyond its city.

To begin, de Boer contacted the local makerspace, in operation for 2.5 years, to find out how things worked. He joined the group and got to know the other members by working on projects with them. Working with the schools was easy because the library already had connections with them. The newest relationship for de Boer was working with local politicians, but it was interesting to see how they understood why the library was pursuing a fab lab. There was a negative response from people within the library community, as more traditional librarians did not understand the project at first. De Boer and his colleagues had them participate in a hands-on session, and this convinced them. They then gave the librarians chances to participate in the project. The whole project really became a grassroots effort that involved many groups and individuals.

A very exciting recent development with FryskLab was the awarding of a grant from a library policy institute in the Netherlands to create modules to help other libraries form fab labs. This work will begin in 2014 and can end up bringing fab labs to all sorts of libraries. The idea for these modules came about as de Boer and his colleagues were thinking about how to connect the library to the hacker movement. As he described it, a key part of their thinking was that libraries had to do more than just buy a 3D printer; they had to have a shared philosophy on why this would be useful to their communities. The modules will help libraries in this process.

Figure 9.6. bus4. *Image provided through a CC BY 2.0 License by FryskLab, http://www.flickr.com/photos/83026924@N03/9762948643*

Who Uses It?

FryskLab is focused on meeting local issues and not on forcing people to come to it, since this might limit access. The focus on local solutions is the most important reason why it joined the international fab lab organization, with another key one being the ability to join a worldwide movement of fab labs to work alongside. Children in de Boer's area of the Netherlands are less fortunate than elsewhere in the country and tend to earn fewer high school diplomas. Companies in the region cannot find qualified people to do their jobs. The hope of FryskLab is to bring technological education to the schools, to familiarize children with these activities, and to inspire them to do something with technology that can affect their futures. The focus of the effort is on economic growth, and it is exciting to pursue this from the perspective of the library. De Boer is very grateful that the library can be used as a platform for the fab lab, and he is curious to see how this influences the development of libraries.

De Boer's group has started to connect with schools and discuss with teachers what FryskLab can do. Teachers were excited by the 3D printer and the positive impact that the fab lab can have, but they also recognized that they need to be able to justify this type of education. De Boer's group applied for a subsidy from a private Dutch fund to develop educational materials to meet the educational goals of the schools. The funds have been received, and the group is developing the programs right now. The curriculum will connect the FryskLab with issues that are important in Friesland. The area has a strong history of being self-sufficient, and bringing these new technologies into education has been easy to connect with this community spirit of DIY. It also has a rich history of

Figure 9.7. 2013-12-11 13.57.25. *Image provided through a CC BY 2.0 License by FryskLab, http://www.flickr.com/photos/83026924@N03/11339612654*

fighting against encroaching water and is doing projects related to this as well as with renewable energy.

Who Supports It?

De Boer and a number of others help out with the logistical and practical aspects of the program. He is not an expert with the equipment and is seeking someone to manage the lab itself. The team has people available who know the equipment and others who are developing the school curriculum. His role is to coordinate these efforts.

What Does It Include?

So far, with the funds that the group has received, it has purchased 3D printers and MaKey MaKeys and is programming with Scratch. In a couple of weeks, the lab will include a laser cutter and soldering stations. All of this fits on the FryskLab bus, along with space to work with the equipment. The group can accommodate 20 students on the bus at one time, and this has worked out well for its trial sessions. It will soon have enough equipment that it can keep items on the bus but also take some into a school to hold a workshop there as well.

How Do You Stay Aware of Developments in Makerspaces?

De Boer's main source is having a good feedreader for blogs and other information. He also recommends being a part of the Dutch makerspace community as a helpful method. He notes that there are so many exciting things going on worldwide, and he recommends keeping your eyes and ears open for new developments. For instance, he watches Kickstarter for new maker projects to get ideas. He also keeps trying to relate maker developments to libraries. Every day is inspiring.

What Is Your Advice to Others Who Would Like to Create a Makerspace?

Try to find out what your local community needs. What are the main issues that you as a library can advance by having a makerspace or fab lab? That has worked well for the FryskLab group. In an urban environment, there are lots of other issues that could be approached: environmental issues, economic problems, or language. There is a fab lab in Utrecht—one of the larger cities in Holland—that works with schools. In a primary school history class, students have to look at a map of the city and then make three new models of streets and parts of the city and print them out in 3D. This connection of 3D printing to the history class brings together history, making, and 21st-century skills. The combination of teaching children how to collaborate and how to solve problems while cooperating with one another really works. People are ready to do this, and you do not have to explain the concept of open access or open source; people know it but need the maker setting to give it a practical impact.

◎ Key Points

3D printing offers a unique creative realm to makers in a library makerspace. It should be seen as more than a fad, with the ability to create practical items.

- 3D printers enable patrons to create physical items from a digital design.
- A wide selection of 3D printers and design software is available, as well as many open collections of designs that can be printed as is or modified.
- 3D printing puts the creation of items into the hands of the maker and may expand to print in plastic and metal.

Now on to some unexpected types of making that library makerspaces are pursuing.

⊚ References

"3D Printer Comparison." 2014. Maker Shed. http://www.makershed.com/Articles.asp?ID=301.

Anderson, Chris. 2012 *Makers: The New Industrial Revolution*. London: Random House Business Books.

Gallant, Riel. 2013. "3D Printing in Libraries Around the World." *3ders* (blog). April 22. http://www.3ders.org/articles/20130422-3d-printing-in-libraries-around-the-world.html.

Gilpin, Lyndsey. 2014. "3D Printing: Ten Factors Still Holding It Back." TechRepublic. February 19. http://www.techrepublic.com/article/3d-printing-10-factors-still-holding-it-back/.

Kemp, Adam. 2013. *The Makerspace Workbench: Tools, Technologies, and Techniques for Making*. Sebastopol, CA: Maker Media.

Lipson, Hod, and Melba Kurman. 2013. *Fabricated: The New World of 3D Printing*. Indianapolis, IN: Wiley.

"The Maker Movement and Its Implications." 2013. *Trends Magazine* 119: 11–16.

Martinez, Sylvia Libow, and Gary Stager. 2013. *Invent to Learn: Making, Tinkering, and Engineering in the Classroom*. Torrance, CA: Constructing Modern Knowledge Press.

O'Neill, Terence, and Josh Williams. 2014. *3D Printing*. Ann Arbor, MI: Cherry Lake.

CHAPTER 10

Resources for the Unexpected: Lesser-Known Making

THIS CHAPTER CONSIDERS SOME INTERESTING POSSIBILITIES for library makerspaces beyond what has already been discussed. The preceding chapters cover many types of making that can happen in libraries. A few others bear mentioning but are harder to categorize. As you consider these types of making, be inspired to imagine other activities that could be added to libraries. There is an amazing number of technologies and activities that people pursue as acts of creation, and a good variety of them are already available in libraries. Creation in libraries comprises a universe of making that includes those activities clearly identified as maker movement staples (3D printers and Arduinos), those of making that already go on in libraries but do not seem like capital-*M* making (quilting and paper crafts), and then those that do not seem to be a part of libraries but actually could be. The book could not end without them, so here they are.

What Your Patrons Could Be Making

The following examples of making are each unique in their nature. They do not easily connect, although there is a bit of a thread in the first few. This may not be so unlike the items in the earlier chapters, but there are fewer shared pieces of equipment or space requirements for them. The "Refills Needed" and "Special Space Requirements" sections that are part of the preceding chapter are missing from this one, and the tools involved in each form of making are briefly mentioned within their descriptions rather than separated out. Again, as you read these, consider that they have all taken place in a library and continue to take place. Maybe they will soon be in your library.

Hog Butchering

The story of a demonstration of hog butchering in the library caught some attention in the media. The event—held at the Johnson County Public Library in Overland, KS—was very successful and attracted 100 people (Bhargava 2012). It is definitely outside the normal mission and programming of public libraries or any type of library (see figure 10.1 for an alternative origami project), and perhaps it is not something that will regularly occur at Johnson County or any other library. But if hog butchering can be done at a library, all sorts of things are possible (Fletcher 2013). There may be larger barriers to cross in terms of what is possible or impossible in a library, but this one seems fairly tall. It will be interesting to see what else library makerspaces attempt going forward. Hog butchering is a real activity that might be of interest to some communities (at least as a demonstration), and it can be an encouragement for adding making of any type. A discussion of tools, techniques, and processes with this activity will be left out of the chapter, except to note that extreme care should be taken in both the cutting and storage of the pork and the disposal of waste products.

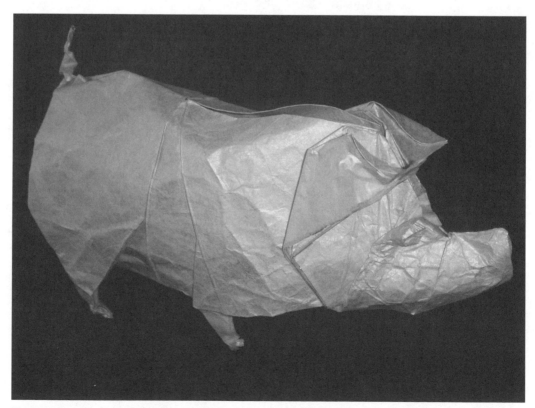

Figure 10.1. Pig (design by Quentin Trollip). *Image provided through a CC BY 2.0 License by Ancella Simoes (Origamiancy), http://www.flickr.com/photos/origamiancy/4619535181*

Cooking

Stepping back a bit from butchery, cooking has a longer history in libraries. There are many ways and reasons to connect your patrons with food and cooking in the library. You might have talented chefs come and demonstrate their cooking, or you might teach kids how to cook or have cooking classes for adults. There might be a focus on preparing healthy meals, canning fruits and vegetables, or making inexpensive meals (Programming Librarian 2014). In the informal survey of library makerspaces, 6 of the 109 respondents (6 percent) indicated that they provided food or culinary arts activities. It is unknown whether the cooking programs connected with these makerspaces predated the creation of the makerspace or were new additions to the library. Regardless, cooking can be a great opportunity to draw people in (everyone loves food!) and teach them something creative that they can pursue in the makerspace or at home. It would be interesting to see if libraries might add microwaves, ovens, and freezers in the same way that they are adding laser cutters and 3D printers.

Kitchen Tool Libraries

Some libraries have taken steps in that direction but with home use of equipment in mind rather than in-library activities. Libraries have typically provided communities with a common store of items to help people access materials that they cannot afford. Those who staff library makerspaces, as noted earlier in the book, have kept this same idea in mind with the technologies and activities that they offer. Types of equipment that libraries can offer are kitchen appliances and other tools. The Toronto Tool Library (not part of the Toronto Public Library) has opened a Kitchen Library to offer its members the loan of kitchen appliances, such as stand mixers and knife sharpeners (Michaelson 2013). The items may be too expensive for someone to buy for occasional use or two bulky to easily store, especially in a smaller kitchen (see examples in figure 10.2). Libraries are well suited to store and lend all sorts of materials and equipment, so why not small appliances? Some precedent in this area has been set by public libraries that lend cake pans (Schwartz 2012) that are large to store and come in specialty designs. It would be interesting to tie lending the means of cooking into makerspace programming on cooking.

Tool Libraries

Moving into more general tools than just kitchen items, there are a number of membership-based tool-lending libraries. They lend items such as concrete saws, tile cutters, and lawn mowers for an annual fee. There is a directory and map of more than 80 tool libraries in North America at http://localtools.org/find/. This could be an approach that libraries could learn from and take on tool lending as a service. The Oakland Public Library has offered a growing tool library since 1991 and has an extensive list of tools and explanation of its policies at http://www.oaklandlibrary.org/locations/tool-lending-library. This again might be a natural outgrowth for a library makerspace—to offer access to equipment within the makerspace itself and then lend out other items for people to use at home.

Tinkering

Tinkering is an activity that a library makerspace can enable, but it is a hard one to clearly define in terms of process, required equipment, or replacement items. For all the structure

Figure 10.2. The new stand mixer. *Image provided through a CC BY 2.0 License by sylvar, http://www.flickr.com/photos/sylvar/76605024*

that there is in people's lives and educational experiences, there is something valuable in activities that operate by the rules of serendipity. Tinkering is an approach to learning that involves just trying things out to see how they work. In doing so, people can take an indirect, experimental path to solving problems or creating things (Resnick and Rosenbaum 2013). It is something that you can intentionally pursue as a way to inspire makers, as well as a natural response that people will have to new technologies.

The informal survey of library makerspaces revealed that 28 respondents (26 percent) support tinkering as an activity. Now this is likely to involve use of items in the makerspace that have other intended purposes. Whether library patrons are children or adults, having an array of resources to work with can allow them to test out making activities or combine various items as needed to solve a problem or make something that interests them. This free-flowing approach to learning is going to be a part of any makerspace, with only the tools available differing. Probably the most useful approach to equipping a library makerspace for tinkering is to have a variety of types of making represented. The interplay of materials can open up people's imaginations and allow tinkering to thrive.

Tinkering might lead into something a bit more defined, such as some of the other areas included on the survey—for example, bicycle building/maintenance (3 respondents, 3 percent), automotive repairs (1 respondent, 1 percent), and guitar repair (1 respondent, 1 percent). There are certainly tinkering aspects to working in these areas, trying out different solutions to problems with bicycles, cars, and guitars. Or, tinkering might lead to practice with making materials and equipment that builds skill and creates a fluid mind that can be applied to various areas. Tinkering involves just trying things out, having fun, and seeing what you can make of a situation or problem (Martinez and Stager 2013).

Minecraft

Minecraft might at first seem like more of an entry in a book on game playing in libraries rather than making in libraries. It certainly deserves a place there as a very popular online and mobile app game. The key element in this game is the making that happens—from small acts, such as digging tunnels as a defensive maneuver, to immense building efforts that re-create parts of our world in the Minecraft world (see one example in figure 10.3). By providing physical space and server space to host Minecraft activities, libraries can support and encourage the creativity that Minecraft players display. This creativity develops players' knowledge and skills in spatial relations, planning, mathematics, and understanding the capacities of the materials used to build items in the games (Hanshaw 2013).

Three library makerspaces profiled in this book have Minecraft-related programming. The Poudre River Public Library (profiled at the end of this chapter) has a Minecraft server set up to let patrons come to the library and play Minecraft together. This is an example of providing easy access to the game for collaborative building efforts and adventures. It is also possible to turn interest in the game into related making activities. The Middletown Free Library (profiled in chapter 4) held a "Minecraft in Real Life" event to create paper crafts, 3D-printed items, and work with circuits (details at http://www.createspacemfl.com/#!programs/c11xt). Minecraft has also inspired library makers to create items to control game movement using MaKey MaKeys, as reported in the profile of the ideaLAB at the Denver Public Library in chapter 8.

Green Making Opportunities

It is possible that another practical area might be ripe for makerspace program development: activities related to gardening, composting, and even farming. There is some

Figure 10.3. Minecraft world created by Philip Burke. *Minecraft ®/TM & © 2009–2013 Mojang / Notch*

evidence that this is a *growing* area for makers. But enough puns—here are some examples that other libraries could build on. The Pima County Public Library in Tucson, AZ, operates a seed library from which patrons can "borrow" seeds, with the hope that they will have a good growing experience and can return seeds from their own plants to the library. More information is available at http://www.library.pima.gov/seed-library, including a list of additional seed libraries across the country. Composting is a very environmentally friendly activity that consists of letting natural items decompose rather than fill up landfills. Holding composting workshops can guide patrons in making their own compost bins; see the one offered by the Northbrook Public Library (IL) at http://www.northbrook.info/event/composting-101. This is certainly a creative act that can revitalize soil and help create more items to enjoy and then compost. This idea of working the land as a form of making has an even more compelling example in the forthcoming creation of the Library Idea Farm makerspace in Old Bridge, NJ (Old Bridge Public Library 2014). The library was recently awarded a grant to create a combination workshop and demonstration garden to combine 3D printing and other maker activities with a community cared-for growing space outside the library. It will be interesting to see how this idea comes together, but it can be expected that it will grow on people.

Button Maker

A creative activity that libraries may already engage in is button making. All that it takes is a button maker (sized for the button you would like to create), the top and bottom of the button (with pin or magnet), a plastic cover, and a paper circle with your image or words. It is very easy to create a template for a button design, as Booth (2011) provides on her blog along with other tips for using buttons in outreach and programs. With the template in hand, it is a simple process to create buttons for patrons or have them choose their own messages or pictures and create their own. This is an easy addition to any library and perhaps the start of more making activities.

Eggbot

A combination of robot and artistic device, the Eggbot did not quite fit into chapters 7 or 8, and so here it sits in chapter 10. The Eggbot can draw with a pen on spheres or egg-shaped items up to the size of a small grapefruit (see figure 10.4). It is programmed with Inkscape software, which allows you to digitally sketch a design that can then be drawn on the object. With a computer, Inkscape software, and the Eggbot, you are ready to create some incredibly artistic eggs, ping-pong balls, or other items. You can use one color at a time, but you can switch pens out after each layer of your design is drawn for a multicolored result. Eggbots are an interesting addition to makerspaces because they combine multiple actions all in one place: do some programming, watch a robot draw, and walk away with a piece of art. More information and kits are available at http://egg-bot.com.

Figure 10.4. Eggbot @ Cal Expo 21. *Image provided through a CC BY 2.0 License by Windell Oskay (oskay), http://www.flickr.com/photos/oskay/4820284466*

Library Makerspace Profile: Berthoud Community Library, Berthoud, CO

http://berthoud.colibraries.org

Sara Wright, Library Director

How Did Your Makerspace Come to Be?

Wright has been reading about the maker movement over the last few years. She was attracted by the base concept of encouraging people to be creators and not just consumers. An important thing that public libraries can do for their communities is to help people find their dreams and their creativity. Patrons check out nonfiction items as half the library's total circulation, and much of it is aimed at teaching them to make or do something. It is an exciting concept to do more than just give them a book and send them home to explore their interests. She started looking at what larger libraries were doing, including the Skokie (IL) Public Library from her home area. Wright wanted to improve the level of technology that the library offered the community, and she realized that they needed to do some space planning to make it work. In particular, they needed to make their available space as flexible as possible. That way, it could be reconfigured as needed for green screen use and other activities. The library encompasses a 5,400-square-foot facility serving a population of 11,000, and Wright manages an annual budget of $300,000.

Even though it is a small library, there is no reason why it could not provide an "on-ramp for people to the bigger maker movement." Wright believes that they can introduce people to the technologies and then, when they need more, she can send them to other local libraries in Loveland or Ft. Collins. These libraries have studio spaces available with advanced forms of making technology. Another strong impetus was that in the Berthoud community, the high school and junior high have several strong robotics teams that have competed and won at the national and international levels. Since there is a demonstrated interest in this area, the library wanted to be able to provide experiences and support in this area even when the schools are closed. They also wanted to offer these resources and experiences to a larger group of kids who cannot be on the robotics teams.

At the start, Wright did not turn to local individuals with making talents. She turned to the Colorado State Library for information on grants that it offered for creation stations. Berthoud did not receive one of the grants, but the state library was able to provide product lists and other resources to help Wright and her staff members choose technologies. Their community has many artists, and they generally focused on creative activities for this reason. They hope to be more involved with local artists as the makerspace develops.

How Do You Market the Makerspace?

Marketing and the media are so fractured, but Wright and her staff pursued every option available to them. They published press releases in the local newspaper and on the library website, but Facebook posts have been the most effective tool for them. They hope to utilize Facebook even more by posting films and stop-motion animations there to show off their technologies. Wright is a big believer in the power of story, and she wants people to know that they can come to the library and try out things that they have only dreamed of using. The word-of-mouth advertising that will come from this marketing and the successful experiences of patrons will keep people excited and keep them coming in. Wright is working with a library intern to create a new brochure on the makerspace with the tagline "Today's tools for tomorrow's dreams." They are still trying to settle on a name for the makerspace.

Who Supports It?

Wright has a staff of seven: three full-time and four part-time. The model that she is working on is to have two or three people on the staff who will learn the technology and be able to help patrons. They are also planning to provide an online learning product such as Lynda.com to help patrons learn how to use the equipment. The staff can then supplement these tutorials with one-on-one support. Wright hopes to find volunteers organically when interested people come to use the equipment and then mention their talents and a willingness to share them.

What Does It Include?

The library just finished its remodeling and had an open house in the last 6 weeks. It has a fast and powerful iMac, Final Cut Pro, and Aperture for video and photo editing, and it purchased a cart for this computer for two people to sit at, which can also easily move around the library. This is the first Mac that it has made available to the library community. It also purchased the following items:

- Adobe Creative Suite for its public PCs
- A portable green screen kit that came with lamps and stands
- A high-end still and video camera
- An audio mixer
- Microphones, headphones, and stands
- HUE animation software and a camera on a bendy tripod
- Manga software
- A scanner
- A VHS-to-DVD converter
- An Epson Artisan printer, which prints up to 13 × 19 in.

The initial focus has been on digital creation and printing. However, Wright and her staff just received a $1,500 grant from a local community fund that they will use for STEM project development. Wright and her youth services librarian will meet with science teachers, the robotics team teacher, and others to see what would be useful.

The flexible part of their plans involves their community room, which can be booked and can now be used for audio and video creation. The rolling Mac cart can go in there, along with much of the other equipment. The space planners that they worked with called this the "lap swim" concept, wherein the spaces that they have can alter purposes, depending on the audience or time of day, much as community swimming pools can be used by adults swimming laps during the day and then by a more diverse audience when kids are home from school.

How Do You Stay Aware of Developments in Makerspaces?

Wright really likes the MakerEd.org and Make.org websites. She has been learning a lot from the general library literature rather than from more technical publications. Articles in *Library Journal* and *Public Libraries Magazine* have been useful. She also reads articles on TechSoup.org.

What Is Your Advice to Others Who Would Like to Create a Makerspace?

Wright believes that having the right philosophy of service makes easily justifies starting a makerspace. Even in the 1990s, Wright started thinking that books were not the library's brand; the stories are. At base level, the public library is not a repository but rather has a role in the community to share ideas and information. Books used to be the main way to do this and the main resource that the library shared. The public library had stuff that people could not afford then, and now, although the sources are not books, people still need access to things that they cannot afford. Clearly, the public library is not dead, since there are people who do not have computers and, even among people who have computers, not everyone has the software or resources that a library can put together in a makerspace. Individuals and businesses in the community should both have the chance to try out stuff before they buy it. Even if you are small, with a little outside-the-box thinking, you can do it! Do not be intimidated by what larger libraries are doing: find the right scale of activities for your library, reach out to other librarians and your state library, and make it happen.

⊙ Library Makerspace Profile: Poudre River Public Library District, Fort Collins, CO

http://www.poudrelibraries.org

Victor Zuniga, Systems Administrator

How Did Your Makerspace Come to Be?

Zuniga and his colleagues started to hear about makerspaces through the American Library Association. The idea appealed to them as a way to engage the community from a different angle. It could allow them to provide education in a different way and get people involved with the library's resources. With the help of the Poudre River Library Trust, the library remodeled one of its branches and created a space called the Collaboration Room, which describes its intended purpose. It has a 42-in. flatscreen television, two laptops, and cables to connect multiple devices to the television. People can sit around the semicircle table in front of the television and display their creations. Other equipment available in the room is a whiteboard, wide-angle webcam, microphone, and headphones. People mostly bring in their own devices (including iPads), or they use the laptops provided by the library.

Who Uses It?

The library has already hosted a number of programs and groups in the room. Groups and small businesses have been looking for a space like this to work in. Entrepreneurs have come in to watch webinars and for videoconferencing via Skype. Students who want to work on projects can meet and create their final projects while discussing the content.

How Do You Market the Makerspace?

The library has held separate open houses for patrons and staff. It wanted to show off the technology and get people thinking about how to use it. However, it ended up with longer conversations during the open house about specific needs that patrons had, and it found patrons making suggestions to meet their own needs and those of others in attendance. The library has used the usual array of marketing efforts, but most people who come to the Collaboration Room come by word of mouth.

Who Supports It?

The Collaboration Room has been very easy for people to use. The library trained the reference desk staff to connect laptops and other devices and to access software for people. Also, it made sure that everyone could log into the library's wireless network.

How Do You Stay Aware of Developments in Makerspaces?

The staff have attended local conferences that have discussed makerspaces. They have spoken with representatives from SparkFun about the options that they could consider for further developing their offerings. It has been a refreshing look at new alternatives for services to offer. Zuniga said that the advice included not necessarily having to establish a dedicated makerspace room but trying to reach out to a wider audience with making activities. Incorporating traditional making such as knitting with more technological making can lead to some interesting combinations.

What Do You See Happening in Your Makerspace in the Next Year?

Zuniga is in the early stages of developing a Minecraft server that will be available to teens in mid-February 2014. It enables a space where teens can create and show what they make to others. The library has been able to use a testing group of teens to help determine what would work and how to structure it. The program is limited to 20 people, with 20 laptops provided by the library. It has been an interesting process in that students are helping one another and they are also helping the library develop this service. The teens feel that they have been listened to and that their expertise has been validated. One of the librarians came up with the idea, and it has appealed to Zuniga and others as an alternative way of learning. He was willing to look into the software and hardware needed to make it happen. He and staff repurposed one of their computers into a server for the game and added a wireless router. They also added security to the system to exclude external players for the present. The students who helped build the server are doing a great job of marketing it to their friends. The library is already getting requests to add a second one once this one is established.

They have thought about adding a 3D printer but have not seen the purpose for having one. If they can find a purpose for a program, though, they will pursue it. Zuniga sees the library as a place for people to gather and learn something together. Why should only Lowes and Home Depot offer how-to programs?

The library will continue to experiment with green screen technology, which it has used in a few programs in 2013. They offered a Day of the Dead (figure 10.5) program for kids in which a staff member dressed up in skull-faced costume, told stories, and then appeared in pictures with each kid. Parents could choose the backgrounds for the pictures, which were changed with the green screen. The program was not focused on the use of the screen, but kids and parents were very impressed with it. Now the library hopes to make the technology more visible in future programs.

What Is Your Advice to Others Who Would Like to Create a Makerspace?

When Zuniga and his colleagues began thinking about makerspaces, they thought in terms of budget. But it is more about taking existing technology and using a new approach or just making small investments. They are interested in offering workshops on adding LED lights to clothing with Raspberry Pi, and they are impressed that you can spend just a little more for the equipment and have a program that really attracts people. Zuniga loves the idea of Minecraft and the ability for players to build whatever they want. He is intrigued by the ability to use it to teach kids academic skills such as math.

Figure 10.5. Day of the Dead Green Screen Program at the Poudre River Public Library. *Image provided by Victor Zuniga*

He hopes to add on to what libraries are offering and to change people's minds about the library and what it can create.

⑥ Key Points

Be open to all kinds of making that could appear in your makerspace. The items in this chapter could be perfect for your makerspace.

- Libraries may wish to lend tools for making as well as host making activities.
- Tinkering is a free-form activity that can inspire makers to greater creativity through experimenting with making tools.
- Minecraft is a popular creative game that can be a part of makerspace activities.

The next chapter examines stages in forming a makerspace.

References

Bhargava, Jennifer. 2012. "Hog Butchering Shows What Else a Library Might Be for These Days." *Kansas City Star* (blog). November 8. http://web.archive.org/web/20130123104619/http://joco913.com/news/hog-butchering-shows-what-a-library-might-be-for-these-day/.

Booth, Char. 2011. "Love Your Library Button Templates (and More): Project Curve, Part One Revisited." *Info-mational* (blog). September 14. http://infomational.wordpress.com/2011/09/14/love-your-library-button-templates-and-more-project-curve-part-one-revisited/.

Fletcher, Owen. 2013. "Check These Out at the Library: Blacksmithing, Bowling, Butchering." *Wall Street Journal Online*. January 7. http://online.wsj.com/news/articles/SB10001424127887324677204578187901423347828.

Hanshaw, Angela. 2013. "Attract Teens to Your Library with Minecraft." *Programming Librarian* (blog). July 25. http://www.programminglibrarian.org/blog/2013/july-2013/attract-teens-to-your-library-with-minecraft.html.

Martinez, Sylvia Libow, and Gary Stager. 2013. *Invent to Learn: Making, Tinkering, and Engineering in the Classroom.* Torrance, CA: Constructing Modern Knowledge Press.

Michaelson, Elizabeth. 2013. "Toronto's Kitchen Library Brings Appliances to All." *Library Journal* (blog). November 5. http://lj.libraryjournal.com/2013/11/library-services/torontos-kitchen-library-brings-appliances-to-all/.

Old Bridge Public Library. 2014. "Old Bridge Public Library Awarded Contract to Build Idea Farm Makerspace." *Old Bridge Public Library* (blog). February 11. http://eastbrunswick.patch.com/groups/old-bridge-public-library/p/old-bridge-public-library-awarded-contract-to-build-idea-farm-makerspace.

Programming Librarian. 2014. "National Culinary Arts Month." http://www.programminglibrarian.org/library/events-and-celebrations/national-culinary-arts-month.html.

Resnick, Michael, and Eric Rosenbaum. 2013. "Designing for Tinkerability." In *Design, Make, Play: Growing the Next Generation of STEM Innovators*, edited by Margaret Honey and David Kanter, 163–81. New York: Routledge.

Schwartz, Meredith. 2012. "Let Them Lend Cake Pans." *Library Journal* (blog). June 14. http://lj.libraryjournal.com/2012/06/library-services/let-them-lend-cake-pans/.

CHAPTER 11

Approaches for Developing a Makerspace That Enables Makers

SO FAR, THE CHAPTERS HAVE CHRONICLED the various ways that you can create a makerspace and the tools that you can use in it, but now it is time to discuss how to ensure that maker activities will work for your library. Chapter 3 discusses the process of forming and operating a makerspace, and the profiles contained in chapters 3 through 10 reveal insights into the many ways that librarians have provided creative spaces for their patrons. This chapter addresses the scale of participation that a library makerspace can move along, whether progressively adding new levels of activity or finding set points that meet community needs at a given moment. It also explores some additional service choices to make when carrying a makerspace forward. Effectively, it answers the question that follows from the preceding seven chapters: what are you going to do in this makerspace with all this maker stuff?

⑥ Stages in Forming a Makerspace

One way to consider this question is to imagine how you might proceed to form your makerspace. This can be imagined as a chronological increase of activities and the ensuing permanence of the space and its services. Good (2013) suggests a set of stages that this development could follow, with the library making the leap from offering traditional library materials and activities to providing making activities. The stages as outlined do illustrate a fairly logical growth pattern for a makerspace. The textbox shows the stages suggested by Good.

Now, not every makerspace will follow the same process of development, by starting at the same place and then growing toward to the ending phase. Makerspaces might start at stage 1 and work their way through to stage 5. Some may start at stage 3 and remain there, and there should be no prejudice shown toward a library that did not "evolve" to the end stage. Every makerspace should try to meet the needs and interests of its community, and that might not lead toward dirty labs or 3D printing.

There is a chart from FutureMakers (2012) that is aimed at those planning library makerspaces. It was inspired by Travis Good, and it serves as a more detailed list of stages or phases for developing a space. A notable aspect of this chart is that it pays attention to the characteristics of the people who will staff the making activities and the people who will be interested in attending programs or working in the space. It also lists for each stage the level of commitment that the library has to assume, in terms of providing or arranging a location and purchasing equipment, moving to a new stage, or continuing to operate at its current level. Again, this may not fit every model of library makerspace, but

---

TEXTBOX 11.1.

MAKERSPACE STAGES

Stage 1: One-off activities. Hold individual workshops or events showcasing a maker activity.

Stage 2: Ongoing meetups. Bring in an existing maker group on a regular basis and hold recurring programs.

Stage 3: Temporary tools and kits. Start to keep maker materials in the library and have them available for collaborative work in the library.

Stage 4: Clean labs. Create a dedicated space in the library that can accommodate some noise and some mild venting of fumes from laser cutters and 3D printers.

Stage 5: Dirty labs. Move to a space where louder and messier activities can happen, such as drilling, woodworking, and metal working (Good 2013).

it does offer some useful suggestions on how to expand makerspace offerings and what impact they might have.

At least a quick word on safety precautions is needed here. As new equipment comes into the makerspace, there needs to be training in using that equipment to be sure that a safe environment is maintained. Private makerspaces tend to require that makers take a class in using a laser cutter or a computer numerical control sewing machine before being able to use it independently. Librarians will need to think about how they will ensure that staff are trained in safe use of equipment and how patrons will be certified as having learned the proper techniques of operation, if they will be allowed to operate the equipment.

◎ Programming for Your Makerspace

A key facet of any makerspace is some sort of programming. Whether it is an occasional workshop or demonstration event to interest people in the space or in the idea of making things or a more involved series of sessions, some thought needs to be given to how the programs will be offered and what options are available. The first question is who will be leading the sessions. In the informal survey of library makerspaces, respondents indicated who teaches training sessions, workshops, or classes in their makerspaces (respondents could choose more than one option). The most popular option was library staff members (chosen by 76 respondents, 70 percent of all respondents), followed by volunteers (42 respondents, 39 percent), paid instructors from beyond the library (20 respondents, 18 percent), and other (18 respondents, 17 percent), which included options such as campus information technology, a center for teaching and learning, and student assistants. It is clear from these results that a blend of instructors should be planned for but also that library staff will likely need to participate. This will have an impact on the training and professional development that must be provided to library staff. It may also mean that the talents and interests of library staff members may guide the library's initial choices of maker activities. Hopefully, volunteers and other experts can be located to enhance or expand those options, either from local makerspaces or from the library's larger community. There is information near the end of this chapter on finding makerspace mentors.

Next, you need to consider what sorts of programs will be offered. Since there are countless topics that could be addressed that will differ depending on the characteristics and audience of the makerspace, here are some general categories of sessions that could be created or pursued:

Demonstration session: an opportunity to show patrons how a particular making technology works or what could be created in the makerspace from a given activity. Could be used to create general interest in the makerspace and to draw people into working on the equipment or activity that is highlighted.

Technology petting zoo: a display of technology items related to making that patrons could try out, with guidance, to gain familiarity with their options. This could be done for a set period, or it could be left in place for a day or multiple days, provided that staff members would be available to assist patrons. This is not unlike a demonstration session in its goals of marketing the makerspace, but it is less structured and very much a hands-on activity.

Figure 11.1. Wordle of library makerspace survey responses on workshops and classes offered.

Instructional workshop: a dedicated session with a mixture of demonstration and hands-on activities to prepare patrons to make things. Generally, the goal would be for patrons to start working on a project that they could return to the makerspace and finish.

A series of workshops and/or demonstrations: this could take a variety of forms, including a number of events on a single making technique that could build in level of difficulty or a calendar of independent events on different making activities, all presented in the course of a 3-month period. The idea would be to have a regular set of programming in place. Patrons could choose to follow the whole series or jump into one area or level depending on their interests.

The teaching role of makerspaces is crucial to identifying and building a helping community that supports all makers. Some combination of these teaching methods will prime the pump for making to happen, and a sustained program of instruction will explore new areas for the development of the space and cause makers' skills to grow. Librarians have the tools and mind-set needed to make this happen, even if they may lack specific making skills. In the informal survey of library makerspaces, respondents were given the opportunity to share the types of workshops or classes that they offer. Figure 11.1 shows a word map of their responses, illustrating the variety of topics.

Programming for Particular Ages and Multiple Ages

The preceding chapters have not made a lot of distinctions about who the audience might be for a given making activity. There are examples given in the makerspace profiles and elsewhere that represent activities and programs aimed at general age groups of participants, particularly school-age children in school and public library makerspaces. Many other activities, from the simplest to the most complex, really could be undertaken by people of any age. The question here is to first consider who you hope to reach with your makerspace and what impact you want it to have. Depending on the makeup of your library community, it might make sense to choose a particular demographic group to pilot the makerspace.

School libraries may have the easiest choice here, given that they primarily serve the students who take classes in the same building or on the same campus. Public libraries have the widest possible range of options on who might come to their programs, leading to a need either to aim programming at specific age ranges or to advertise events only to certain groups. Academic libraries will generally focus on students at their institutions but will likely reach out to faculty and staff members and may serve adults and others in their community. Once you identify who your audience is, you can sculpt programs to fit the individuals whom you hope to reach. You could, for instance, focus the makerspace and your programming on teens. As some of the makerspaces profiled in this book have found (see the Allen County Public Library in chapter 5 and the Denver Public Library in chapter 8), that may lead to adults becoming interested in the makerspace, which can lead to an expansion of the makerspace or the creation of a whole new area for adults (if funding and space are available).

The situation to prepare for is one in which you are offering a makerspace with open hours for anyone to come in and use the materials and equipment. If it is truly open for anyone, you need to be ready for experienced makers to come in alongside families with toddlers. It is more of a question of having age-appropriate activities and guidance available to meet the need. Hard age restrictions ("only available for patrons 12 and older") might make sense in some settings, such as using woodworking equipment or laser cutters, while ability may be the better deciding factor in others. That gets back to the idea of having required classes or training for using some equipment independently. Generally, you want to have an environment in which people have opportunities for making that fit their skill levels and interests. You may need to subdivide your programming to make that happen.

◉ Moving toward a Space That Is Open, Dirty, Noisy, or Dedicated

The decision on whether and how to expand a popular service is a regular part of library work, and makerspaces fit well into this framework. As interest grows in the makerspace, there will be calls to add types of making or to change the way the current items are made available. Looking back at the suggested stages at the beginning of this chapter, there are four key transitions that a library makerspace might want to make: open labs, dirty labs, noisy activities, dedicated spaces. All of these require a deeper commitment to the makerspace in that you are being called on to have library space used in particular ways for particular purposes. To make these transitions, you will need to take the makerspace seriously and show a greater intention to continue it as a service. Each of the four transitions is listed here, with a brief discussion on how it affects the library and the provision of the makerspace.

Open Lab

An *open lab* refers to having the makerspace or maker equipment available for patrons to use outside of specific class or workshop times. It might be a set time frame each day or just on certain days in the week. An open lab requires that library staff members or volunteers are available to assist people using the space, and it is predicated on there being enough interested makers to justify having that staffing available. Depending on the types of activities available, having an open lab might mean that the makerspace will need a dedicated space if it does not have one already. Or, any number of activities could be moved into a meeting room, a classroom within the library, or even an open seating area during the set times for open work. The important thing about having open work time in making is that it allows for unstructured work to happen and for makers to discover new things about the tools and processes they are using. Tinkering can truly happen in an open lab.

Dirty Lab

As noted at the start of this chapter, a dirty lab is a makerspace that accommodates messy activities such as woodworking or painting or cooking. Many maker activities can be pulled out and used in whatever space is available and then put away again. Lots of making can be messy, but the level of mess and relative ease of cleanup can keep making such as paper crafts, sewing, and 3D printing outside a dirty lab. With dirty lab activities, you are also likely to need dedicated space to keep equipment in place. Beyond just finding or creating a walled-off space, the furnishings, flooring, and facilities of the space should accommodate the making that is going to happen. If tables and chairs would be helpful to the making work, they should be able to stand up to the dirt created and be easily cleaned. Carpet must yield to more easily cleaned flooring. The requisite electrical outlets, lighting, and other added items should be installed, such as a sink to aid with cooking activities.

Noisy Activities

Noisy activities could describe various makerspace actions, from using any sort of cutting device to having a boisterous group of middle schoolers work with circuits. The primary thought here, though, is accommodating making that produces sound that is essential to the process but likely to distract others. This could just as easily describe audio-recording activities, such as the drum kit mentioned back in chapter 7, as well as the whine of drills and computer numerical control routers and the whirr of sewing machines. A space needs to have noise-cancellation or sound-dampening panels in place to work as a recording studio or a workroom. Dealing with noise and containing sound are huge issues and ones that must be addressed to keep makerspaces viable in a library environment (Bagley 2013).

Dedicated Spaces

A dedicated space, as noted in the other three transitions, is pretty much a requirement for a makerspace to take on the next level of activities or to have a chance to expand beyond occasional programming. Once again, as with the stages of development discussed earlier, there is no requirement that a library take on noisy or dirty activities or attempt to offer an open lab environment. Makerspaces can remain entirely mobile enterprises and move into action inside and beyond the library as programming needs dictate. But a permanent space, even one that is not perfectly outfitted for every possible use, gives the makerspace a sense of freedom and something of an anchored feeling. That space is helpful for holding programs that can be separate from the rest of the library and for storing items and equipment. Projects can be left unfinished in situ so that makers can return to them. Establishing a space for the makerspace is also a useful way to test out the limits of making possibilities within the library and to plan for either improving that space or building a new one.

ⓖ Going Mobile

Calling something a makerspace appears to presume that the making is happening in a set-aside space, like the dedicated space just discussed. Another way to look at this is that the making is happening somewhere in some space, even if that space is only temporarily focused on making. This is the concept behind the mobile makerspace experience, in which the making tools are brought to the space, used there, and then packed up and moved elsewhere for storage. The temporary space might be inside the library, outdoors, at a school, or anywhere in the community where you wish to bring it and someone agrees to have you making stuff. The mobile makerspace could involve a range of technologies, given that laptops and 3D printers are fairly mobile. It is an attempt to bring making to the people.

Thinking out the possibilities, the mobile makerspace might be the way that you start off with making activities in the library, bringing things out when needed into a shared common space and then returning them until the next program. The mobile makerspace might be a way to take some of the making activities from a dedicated space elsewhere, say, to a branch of a multilocation library system (see the Johnson County Public Library profile in chapter 8). Or it might be the only way that you offer making, as in the case of the Louisville Free Public Library, which has no central makerspace (Owens 2013). Or the makerspace might be located in a bus that you drive to wherever making needs to happen (see the FryskLab fab lab description in chapter 9). Rassette (2014) offers a description of a low-tech collection of art supplies that she uses in a public library with teens. Hilton (2013) provides details on a more technology-focused mobile makerspace using MaKey MaKeys that has a more surprise-focused implementation. This mobile concept can be more than just an introduction to making and is an option to pursue if it would fit your library.

ⓖ Making at Home

Speaking of getting makerspace materials on the move, some libraries are trying out the option of circulating maker-oriented items. On the one hand, this seems to work against some of the community-building and peer-guiding elements of a makerspace that works in a co-located space. On the other, circulating makerspace items follows a very traditional library model for getting things that people cannot buy into their hands to use. Someone who learns about a technology at a library makerspace event can then go home with that technology and make something.

Now, what are libraries circulating? The University of British Columbia Library lends Arduinos for a 3-day loan. The North Carolina State University Hunt Library circulates 3D scanners and MaKey MaKeys (see chapter 9 for the library makerspace profile). Many public and academic libraries are lending iPads and digital cameras and could add more maker-focused items.

There are a variety of electronics kits available that libraries could purchase and check out. One difficulty is that many of these kits are intended for a single a project. Even those that are reusable can be tricky for library staff to check back in and know what might be missing (Good 2013). This will likely get easier as more kits are produced with reuse in mind.

◎ Having Makerspace Mentors and Makers in Residence

The presence of volunteers in makerspaces can be a huge help to lend support to other makers. Volunteers or mentors can teach classes, staff open times at the makerspace, or just assist patrons while working on their own projects. Mentors may come from a variety of backgrounds. They may be associated with a local makerspace, a hackerspace, or another making-related group, or they may just be individuals in the community with skills that they would like to share. As you plan your makerspace and talk with people in the community, you may meet individuals who could serve in a mentoring role. The "Makerspace Playbook" (Makerspace.com 2013) has some guidance for creating a mentor interest survey. There may also be the opportunity to make a more formal arrangement with one or more mentors and establish a maker-in-residence program (Ginsberg 2013). This can bring a set of skills into the library that really adds to the community of your makerspace. The maker in residence could teach, demonstrate past and ongoing projects, and help patrons move toward making their own creations. The period of residence could be for a few workshops or for a longer period. The Westport (CT) Library's maker in residence in early 2014 was on hand for a 2-month period (Westport Library 2014).

◎ Holding Your Own Mini–Maker Faire or Maker Camp

Maker faires are immensely popular events in the maker movement. The Bay Area Maker Faire drew more than 120,000 people in 2013 (Nagata 2013). Maker faires offer chances for makers to show off their creations and their techniques. *Make:* magazine sponsors some of the largest faires (http://makerfaire.com), and a number of cities and regions have smaller events. These faires are great opportunities for libraries to market their makerspaces, to connect with other people who are interested in making, and to perhaps find interested mentors. In addition, the library could hold its own mini–maker faire or maker day, in which the work of patron makers could be shown off and making activities demonstrated. Martinez and Stager (2013) offer a chapter with guidance on creating a making day in a school setting, but many of the elements would work in any library setting.

Another *Make:*-created opportunity is the annual Maker Camp (http://makezine .com/maker-camp), which is held each summer. The free event lasts for 30 days, and on each day, there will be a new product created. Videos on how to make the products are broadcast on Google Hangouts, and there are opportunities to interact with the maker camp counselors. Interested makers are provided with lists of materials so that they can plan ahead. It is a great source of making curriculum for you to use as you hold a summer making program (such as working with Arduinos, as shown in figure 11.2). You could structure a daily or weekly meeting to go over one or more projects and have this help kick off your own programming or supplement existing programming that you are doing.

Figure 11.2. Intro to Arduino. *Image provided through a CC BY 2.0 License by SparkFunElectronics, http://www.flickr.com/photos/sparkfun/8167729010*

You can also sign up to be an affiliate site for Maker Camp (at no charge), which will share your location through its website so that makers in your area can find you. The CreateSpace of the Middletown Public Library (profiled in chapter 4) did this in 2013 and had an excellent experience with it.

Listen to Your Makers and Those Who Have Gone Before

With all the decisions that you have to make on programming and expanding the capabilities of your space, it is crucial to look to two sources for information. They are the same sources that you used when gathering input on how to start the space, and they are just as important as the makerspace continues. First, be sure to talk to your makers and take the pulse of their making activities and their happiness with the space. You may follow some of the same routes you did when surveying potential makers or just touch base with individuals on occasion. You want to make sure that their needs are being met and that the space continues to interest them. It is also very important to watch and see if new people are coming to your programming and dropping into the space. You want to make sure that the makerspace is not becoming a closed circle but one that is growing and taking in new people and new challenges.

Second, keep listening to the wisdom of those who have preceded you in creating library makerspaces or those who are newly coming alongside you. That advice was helpful as you created your own plan and story for what a library makerspace could be. Now you can use those articles, websites, or conversations to keep on track and continue to succeed. Stay aware of new trends in technology and new applications in makerspace environments. The resources in chapter 12 will help you stay on track. Be sure to not just watch for new stuff but try new things out. And the knowledge from the maker movement and library maker community should lead you back to your patrons to see what they think of these possibilities.

🌀 Key Points

Library makerspaces offer many programming and service possibilities.

- There are several stages or transitions that library makerspaces can go through.
- Workshops, trainings, and classes can be taught by library staff, volunteers, or paid instructors from beyond the library.
- There are several types of training sessions to choose from.
- Makerspaces can be mobile, and making can happen at home with circulating maker technologies.
- Identifying maker mentors and establishing makers-in-residence programs can add guidance, coordination, and enthusiasm to your makerspace programs.
- Maker faires, mini–maker faires, and Maker Camp are great opportunities to inspire library staff and patrons and to teach skills.

Now, the book concludes with a chapter on keeping track of makerspace happenings and considering how the library can alter its role to include makerspaces.

🌀 References

Bagley, Caitlin A. 2013. "Jeff Sturges on Libraries and Makerspaces." *ALA TechSource* (blog). February 15. http://www.alatechsource.org/blog/2013/02/jeff-sturges-on-libraries-and-makerspaces.html.

FutureMakers. 2012. "What Is Your Readiness for a Makerspace?" http://kidsmakethingsbetter.com/wp-content/uploads/2013/11/What-is-your-level-of-makerspace-readiness.pdf.

Ginsberg, Sharona. 2013. "Mentors for Makers: Effective and Budget-Friendly." *MakerBridge* (blog). December 16. http://makerbridge.si.umich.edu/blog/131216-800

Good, Travis. 2013. "Making Makerspace Libraries." ILEADUSA2013. YouTube. March 28. http://www.youtube.com/watch?v=WV_Eu5Kz1cA&feature=youtu.be.

Hilton, Lisa. 2013. "Guerrilla Maker Space: An Interview with Emerging Designers." *Makezine* (blog). December 10. http://makezine.com/magazine/guerrilla-maker-space-an-interview-with-emerging-designers/.

Makerspace.com. 2013. "Makerspace Playbook." http://makerspace.com/wp-content/uploads/2013/02/MakerspacePlaybook-Feb2013.pdf.

Martinez, Sylvia Libow, and Gary Stager. 2013. *Invent to Learn: Making, Tinkering, and Engineering in the Classroom.* Torrance, CA: Constructing Modern Knowledge Press.

Nagata, Kazuaki. 2013. "Hands on with the 'Maker Movement.'" *Japan Times.* June 26. http://www.japantimes.co.jp/life/2013/06/26/lifestyle/hands-on-with-the-maker-movement/#.UxSqUPldVuI.

Owens, Tammi. 2013. "Notes from LITA Forum 2013, Session 1." *Hundreds of Things* (blog). December 1. http://www.hundredsofthings.net/notes-from-lita-forum-2013-session-1/.

Rassette, Eden. 2014. "Easy Does It: A Pop-Up Teen Makerspace." *Library as Incubator Project* (blog). February 3. http://www.libraryasincubatorproject.org/?p=13181.

Westport Library. 2014. "Maker-in-Residence." http://westportlibrary.org/maker-residence.

CHAPTER 12

Remaking the Library? Tracking the Present and Future of Making in Libraries

MAKERSPACES ARE IN LIBRARIES. They are meeting a variety of needs and creating interest among people who use those libraries and have now come into contact with making. The spread of makerspaces of any kind was nearly invisible even 5 years ago, and now the library community is making makerspaces appear in many settings. The future of these new spaces is understandably unclear, but it is possible to examine where their creators might take them and how this can influence the future of libraries and the future of making. This chapter examines some key questions about the making activities supported by libraries, considers the impact of maker developments in the wider world, and examines tools that librarians can use to track makerspace developments and connect with colleagues worldwide.

Building the Future of Makerspaces

The growth of library makerspaces to date has been rapid. There are many libraries and communities that do not yet have makerspaces (Colegrove 2013), but as these new spaces appear, it will be interesting to watch how they develop. Every new makerspace is the result of a combination of local needs and influences from the wider network of makers. They are not exact copies of earlier models, and even if they start in a mode driven by work elsewhere, they cannot remain static. Each makerspace has the potential to do something transformative with making activities and then influence that wider network. You can expect that the makerspaces of today will continue to evolve as their numbers swell. New technologies will come, and older ways of making will continue to be rediscovered and perhaps refined or altered by technology and new approaches.

One meaningful impact will not be exclusively technological but rather social. Although makerspaces are available in many libraries for people of all ages, there is a significant focus on providing learning opportunities for children. As school library makerspaces grow, the opportunities for students to participate in making activities will grow beyond the options that they might have in art, science, and shop classes. If children are increasingly working on STEM and STEAM projects in the library and in classrooms, they will join a larger audience of people who might be interested in making things on an ongoing basis. There are growing parallels between educational goals and standards and the goals and principles of makerspaces (Gustafson 2013). Will growing numbers of kids who have experienced making be more likely to pursue makerspace experiences at their schools, in their public libraries, and on college campuses? That might happen. Books such as the one by Roslund and Rogers (2014) may also help move this interest forward and have a ripple effect on multiple libraries and on the world as a whole.

When you look to the future, it is often hard to see beyond the next week or the next fiscal year. Given the immediacy of this view and the expectations that it allows, it is still possible to see if a broader sense of the future can be deduced from expressed needs. In chapter 4, there is a section on what is missing from the makerspaces in the informal survey of makerspaces in libraries. In that section, respondents suggested five categories of things that they would like to add to their makerspaces in the coming year. Here are those categories (in order of popularity):

- 3D printers
- Arts and crafts or handmade items
- More space or dedicated space
- More workshops and public events
- 3D scanners

There is a nice blend in these categories of high technology along with lower-level but high-skill technologies. You can also see representation of the stuff that people use for making along with the space to use it in. What ties this all together is the hope for additional events that bring people together to learn about making and demonstrate what they have made. If this says anything about the future of makerspaces in libraries, it is perhaps that the libraries of the moment are focused on expanding their making options, finding more room to make things, and teaching more people how to make. If that is what can be expected from library makerspaces in the future, then this experiment will become all the more substantial in presence and reach.

One huge expected development with making tools is that they could eventually enable a makerspace or a home user to create and repair many products without turning to manufacturers or retailers. It may be that small networks of individuals and makerspaces could trade products back and forth, setting up an alternative economy. Many items could be repaired by printing or cutting spare parts (Thompson and Goldberg 2013). Will making tools and shared designs lead to individuals making all their own stuff, including spare parts, and decreasing the need for centralized manufacturing (Lipson and Kurman 2013)? Will maker devices grow cheap and flexible enough to handle a wide range of products? In turn, will individual makers need the library? Again, this future is not clear, but developments with 3D printers and computer numerical control machines make the world created by Cory Doctorow (2009) in his novel *Makers* look like a distinct possibility: a world where individual makers use shared designs to create products that they then print and use or send out to home 3D printers on demand. What libraries can do to support such efforts and whether libraries have a role in that world has yet to be confronted but will come in time.

This is not to say that everyone will have a positive response to these developments or even understand what a makerspace is or why the library has it. Library makers must expect that makerspaces will be questioned in their communities and will not have an easy road to universal acceptance. All makers must be prepared with a good explanation for why a makerspace is in the library and not elsewhere in the community or on the campus (James 2013). Chapter 2 discusses some reasons for having a makerspace at all, particularly in the library. The other activity that can be helpful here is to continue to educate administrators and stakeholders on what the larger maker movement is all about (Shapiro 2013). If you are sure that you are doing the right thing, be ready to explain that to others.

Sharing Library Users' Stuff and Making Their Own

What can libraries do with a makerspace that other entities cannot? Two things: first, serve as a mechanism to share the created items on behalf of patrons; second, make stuff that improves library services. On the first point, libraries are well suited to being physical and virtual repositories for stuff. Does the library become a place for its makers to display what they have made or to share the open source creations that they wish to offer the world? It is unclear what this might look like, but LaRue's (2013) vision of the library as publisher might help establish a structure toward supporting the creative efforts of patrons (recruiting authors and reviewers, serving as a market for copies of the book, etc.). In a makerspace-related example, the Fayetteville Free Library Fab Lab has programs for children to create their own books, which the library catalogs and circulates (Britton 2012). There is a great analogy related to making—namely, whether the library should be a grocery store, where people get the information bits they need, or a kitchen, where people put the information together in a final product (Valenza 2008). Is there a way for a library to also be a dining room or a restaurant, where people beyond the library and other than the maker come to use and maybe even buy the end product?

On the second point, there are at least two good reasons for library staff members to get into making beyond their role of supporting a makerspace for others. Modeling creation will help staff understand the activities and technologies involved and can provide an example for their patrons and the larger community of makers. Focusing their creative efforts on library-related problems or needs can help them improve or expand their services in some way. There are some interesting examples in the projects list and blog at http://www.librarytestkitchen.org, and this is only the beginning of possibilities. As libraries begin to host makerspaces, the interplay of maker culture and library culture should lead to some intriguing developments.

As the makerspaces-in-libraries movement continues to grow, information sources are needed to stay aware of larger trends and to follow up on specific technologies and project ideas. Fortunately, there is a large number of websites, electronic discussion groups, and other resources available for making and makerspaces in general and library makerspaces. The following list of resources, while far from complete, was compiled through investigations and the suggestions of respondents to the informal survey of makerspaces in libraries (see the appendix for details). Martinez and Stager (2013) also have an extensive list of resources at the end of their book that is worth a look, although they are more focused on K–12 making activities.

General Makerspace Resources

Make: (http://makezine.com): The website for *Make:* magazine contains a blog, videos, project information, and links to the other Maker Media sites. The projects are sorted by category and rated for difficulty.

Maker book lists (http://jocolibrary.bibliocommons.com/lists/show/98731951_jclmeredithn): A series of maker book lists created by Meredith Nelson, Johnson County Public Library, organized by age and by type of making. A great place to track down some maker titles for your library collection.

Maker Education Initiative (http://www.makered.org): Sponsored by Maker Media, Intel, Cognizant, and Pixar, the Maker Education Initiative is dedicated to getting kids making. There are free resources provided on the site to help plan programs.

Maker Faire (http://makerfaire.org): Advertises maker faires and provides information on taking part in them. It is a very helpful way to find a maker event near you.

The Maker Mom (http://www.themakermom.com): A blog that highlights making resources, especially focused on STEM resources for kids.

YOUmedia Network (http://www.youmedia.org): YOUmedia manages digital learning labs for youth in a variety of locations. They offer a toolkit for forming a makerspace program and links to resources that can help in the planning process.

Makerspace Directories

Makerspace.com has a directory of makerspaces at http://makerspace.com/maker space-directory, and the *Make:* magazine site has a list of maker community groups at http://makezine.com/maker-community-groups. The MakerMap (http://themakermap.com) is an open-source directory of making organizations and sites that provides a searchable Google Maps interface to help you locate local and regional makers. Similar sources include Hackerspaces (http://hackerspaces.org/wiki/List_of_Hackerspaces) and MIT's Fab Lab List (http://fab.cba.mit.edu/about/labs).

Library-Focused Maker Resources

Build-a-Lab Digital Media Lab Training Series (http://heritage.utah.gov/library/build-a-lab): This site hosts a series of four archived webinars sponsored by the Utah State Library in 2014 on digital media labs and makerspaces around the United States. Provides information on how the labs were created and the services they offer.

Library as Incubator Project (http://www.libraryasincubatorproject.org): This blog highlights the connections between artists and libraries and shares creative opportunities and resources.

Library Makers (http://librarymakers.blogspot.com): A blog dedicated to promoting making projects, particularly ones aimed toward children and focused on arts and crafts.

Library Makerspaces (http://www.pinterest.com/cari_young/library-makerspaces): This is a Pinterest board with links to many maker projects and products. It is a great way to browse for projects.

Make It at the Library—Makerspace Resources (http://libraries.idaho.gov/make-it-at-the-library): A collection of makerspace examples, funding resources, and making materials created by the Idaho Commission for Libraries.

MakerBridge (http://makerbridge.si.umich.edu): This site offers discussion forums for people working in library makerspaces, as well as a blog and lists of recommended tools for making.

Makers (http://www.nekls.org/nekls-services/makers): This lengthy list of resources on makerspaces and making devices and projects was created by the Northeast Kansas Library System.

Makerspaces (http://youthserviceslibrarianship.wikispaces.com/Makerspaces): An excellent collection of makerspace resources created by students in the University of Illinois Graduate School of Library and Information Science as part of a larger wiki entitled "Youth Services Librarianship: A Guide to Working with Young People in School and Public Libraries."

Technology Toolbox (http://libraryguides.oswego.edu/toolbox): A guide filled with resources on presentations, multimedia production, and 3D printing, developed by Emily Thompson at the State University of New York at Oswego.

Project Sites

Adafruit Learning System (http://learn.adafruit.com): This site is a collection of tutorials and project ideas for working with Arduino, Raspberry Pi, Lilypad, circuits, 3D printing, and more.

Cubeecraft (http://www.cubeecraft.com): A collection of paper craft patterns of various types that can be printed for folding.

Instructables.com (http://www.instructables.com): Instructables is the place to find project instructions to make all sorts of things. If something can be made, there is probably a video here on how to make it. You can also post your own projects here.

Make It at Your Library (http://makeitatyourlibrary.org): A cooperative project of ILEAD USA graduates (a library leadership program) and Instructables.com, the site offers various types of making projects. The projects can be sorted by topic, age level, time to complete, and cost.

Thingiverse (http://thingiverse.com): This site is a repository of 3D designs that are open for anyone to modify or print using a 3D printer. You can find additional 3D design collections in chapter 9.

Maker Products

Afinia (http://www.afinia.com): Information on using your Afinia 3D printer and a gallery of printed projects.

Arduino (http://arduino.cc): Offers project information and support for using Arduinos.

MakerBot (http://makerbot.com): The 3D printer vendor site offers many bits of advice on 3D printing along with information on its products.

Maker Shed (http://makershed.com): The official store of *Make:* magazine.

Materials, Tools, and Kits (http://libraries.idaho.gov/page/materials-tools-and-kits): A lengthy list of maker products with links to purchase them or learn more about them.

Raspberry Pi (http://raspberrypi.org): The site provides projects and support to use with Raspberry Pi.

SparkFun Electronics (http://www.sparkfun.com): A great place to shop for electronic gadgets, including items for e-textiles, robotics, circuits, and Raspberry Pis. The company offers educator kits, which are bulk amounts of materials to get a whole class making.

Makerspace Funding and Donation Sources

Donors Choose (http://www.donorschoose.org): A site for public school teachers to post their classroom needs and then see if donors will choose to fund them. It could be a resource for your school library makerspace to seek some equipment.

Institute of Museum and Library Services—Learning Labs in Libraries and Museums (http://www.imls.gov/about/learning_labs.aspx): A series of grant programs offered to help create digital learning labs in libraries and museums, with links to successfully funded programs and resources related to digital literacy and projects.

TechSoup (http://www.techsoup.org): An organization that collects donated technology from partner organizations and distributes it to nonprofit organizations and libraries.

Discussion Lists

Create (http://www.cvl-lists.org/mailman/listinfo/create): The Create list is designed for those working with library makerspaces.

K–12 Digital Fabrication Labs (bit.ly/k12fablabgroup): This Google Group is primarily aimed at K–12 makerspaces and maker activities.

Librarymakerspace-l (http://lists.ufl.edu/cgi-bin/wa?A0=LIBRARYMAKER-SPACE-L): A discussion list for librarians with library makerspaces.

Twitter Hashtags and Folks to Follow

The following list shows Twitter (http://twitter.com) hashtags, search terms, and Twitter accounts to follow for information on making. There are many more out there, depending on your specific making interests, but these will get you started:

#3Dprinting

#librarymakerspace

#maker

#makers

#makerspace (with or without "library")

#STEMchat

"makerspace"

@make

@makerbridge

@makered

@makezine

Facebook Groups

There are two groups with a specific focus on library makerspaces. You can find similarly minded individuals here to share your makerspace questions:

Makerspaces and the Participatory Library, https://www.facebook.com/groups/library maker

Vermont Libraries as Makerspaces, https://www.facebook.com/groups/4417199392 68502

General Technology Sites and Blogs

ALA TechSource (http://www.alatechsource.org/blog): The American Library Association's TechSource blog provides discussions on many technologies used in libraries and elsewhere, and it has covered makerspace developments in libraries.

Boing Boing (http://boingboing.net): A blog that features all sorts of interesting stories about technology and culture. Covers topics that might be of interest to makers, including ones that directly mention makers and makerspaces.

EDUCAUSE (http://educause.edu): A site and blog focused on developments in technology that affect higher education.

Engadget (http://engadget.com): A site and blog for news and reviews on many technology products.

Gizmodo (http://gizmodo.com): A site and blog for stories about technology news and products.

Mashable (http://mashable.com): A site and blog for news and resources related to our digital world.

The Next Web (http://thenextweb.com): A blog focused on international technology news.

ReadWrite (http://readwrite.com): A technology news blog.

Wired (http://www.wired.com): A blog for *Wired* magazine, which reports on many technology issues including online resources.

⊚ Passing the First Mile Marker on the Journey

This book chronicles the rise of makers and the inclusion of maker activities in the work of libraries. This is a new service and a new reason for libraries to provide equipment, space, and programming. Time will tell if makerspaces will last in libraries, be better placed in larger communities of makers, or fade altogether. What seems certain is that as long as people are curious about how things work, they will take them apart and try to make them work again, work better, or work differently. As this process continues, people will gain skills that they can pass on to others. Making will not end, nor will the teaching and sharing of making knowledge. As libraries continue in their mission as community-gathering spaces dedicated to the sharing of knowledge, it seems well in keeping with this mission to provide the means to make, the space to gather in, and the access to the knowledge that keeps making happening. Libraries should investigate making and see what they can provide to help their communities.

⊚ Key Points

- The future of library makerspaces appears bright if they pursue equipment, space, and community-building events as needed parts of makerspaces.
- Libraries should seek ways to apply their traditional skills to serve makers and develop new library products by accepting the challenge of applying making.
- There are many resources to turn to for more information on many aspects of library makerspaces.

References

Britton, Lauren. 2012. "A Fabulous Laboratory." *Public Libraries* 52 (4): 30–33.

Colegrove, Tod. 2013. "Editorial Board Thoughts: Libraries as Makerspace?" *Information Technology & Libraries* 32 (1): 2–5.

Doctorow, Cory. 2009. *Makers*. New York: Tor.

Gustafson, Ellen. 2013. "Meeting Needs: Makerspaces and School Libraries." *School Library Monthly* 29 (8): 35–36.

James, Joseph. 2013. "Another Story. Common Ground." *American Libraries* 44 (11/12): 22.

LaRue, James. 2013. "Wanna Write a Good One? Library as Publisher." *American Libraries* (blog). June 25. http://www.americanlibrariesmagazine.org/article/wanna-write-good-one-library-publisher.

Lipson, Hod, and Melba Kurman. 2013. *Fabricated: The New World of 3D Printing*. Indianapolis, IN: Wiley.

Martinez, Sylvia Libow, and Gary Stager. 2013. *Invent to Learn: Making, Tinkering, and Engineering in the Classroom*. Torrance, CA: Constructing Modern Knowledge Press.

Roslund, Samantha, and Emily Puckett Rodgers. 2014. *Makerspaces*. Ann Arbor, MI: Cherry Lake.

Shapiro, Phil. 2013. "A Librarian's Guide to Boosting the Maker Movement." Makezine.com. August 28. http://makezine.com/2013/08/28/a-librarians-guide-to-boosting-the-maker-movement/.

Thompson, Clive, and Carin Goldberg. 2013. "The Fixer Movement Repair All Your Broken Stuff, Save the World." *Wired* 21 (7): 74.

Valenza, Joyce. 2008. "Library as Domestic Metaphor." *Neverending Search* (blog). August 25. http://blogs.slj.com/neverendingsearch/2008/08/25/library-as-domestic-metaphor/.

Appendix: Makerspaces in Libraries Survey

ⓖ Overview

During October and November 2013, I conducted a web-based survey on makerspaces in libraries. It was created as a form in Google Drive. Librarians were asked to respond anonymously. The survey was distributed through Twitter, a Facebook group (Makerspaces and the Participatory Library), and the following list of library electronic discussion groups:

- ARLIS-L@lsv.arlisna.org, Art Libraries Society of North America
- cjc-l@ala.org, ACRL Community and Junior Colleges Section
- code4lib@listserv.nd.edu, Coders for libraries discussion
- COLLIB-L@ala.org, ACRL College Libraries Section
- create@cvl-lists.org, Discussion of creation and makerspaces in libraries
- lis-pub-libs@jiscmail.ac.uk, UK Public Libraries
- lita-l@ala.org, Library and Information Technology Association
- lm_net@listserv.syr.edu, School Library Media and Network Communications
- publib@webjunction.org, OCLC Public Librarianship
- sla-dite@sla.lyris.net, Special Libraries Association–IT Division
- uls-l@ala.org, ACRL University Libraries Section
- web4lib@listserv.nd.edu, Web Technologies in Libraries

There were 143 respondents. In response to the question "Does your library provide a makerspace or a similar space?" 58 (41 percent) of the respondents answered yes, 51 (36 percent) are planning to start makerspaces in the near future, and 34 (24 percent) are not currently providing makerspaces nor are planning to do so. The following responses all come from the 109 librarians who currently provide makerspaces or who plan to soon start a makerspace. Their responses to each of the 14 questions are summarized as follows.

ⓖ Survey Questions

"What Type of Library Do You Work In?"

Table A.1. "What Type of Library Do You Work In?"

	RESPONDENTS	
	n	%
Public	55	51
Academic	38	36
School	10	9
Other	4	4
Special	0	0

"Where Is Your Library Located (State/Province/Country)?"

Librarians from 30 U.S. states responded to the survey along with librarians from seven other countries: Australia (1), Canada (2), China (1), Denmark (1), Japan (1), the Netherlands (1), and the United Kingdom (4).

Table A.2. "Where Is Your Library Located?"

STATE	RESPONDENTS, *n*	STATE	RESPONDENTS, *n*
Alabama	1	North Carolina	5
Arizona	1	North Dakota	1
California	5	New Jersey	3
Colorado	7	New York	5
Connecticut	1	Ohio	4
Florida	2	Oklahoma	5
Georgia	3	Oregon	1
Idaho	3	Pennsylvania	2
Illinois	3	South Carolina	3
Indiana	3	Tennessee	1
Kansas	5	Texas	8
Louisiana	1	Utah	1
Massachusetts	5	Virginia	5
Michigan	4	Washington	4
Missouri	2	Wisconsin	1

"What Do You Call Your Makerspace?"

A selection of these comments is included in chapter 3.

"How Long Has Your Space Been in Place?"

Makerspaces tend to be a new addition to most respondents' libraries. The *other* responses came from respondents who had not yet started to offer a makerspace.

Table A.3. "How Long Has Your Space Been in Place?"

YEARS	RESPONDENTS	
	n	%
< 1	46	46
1–2	13	13
2–3	5	5
3–4	2	2
> 4	4	4
Other	29	29

"Did the Funding to Start Your Makerspace Come From . . . ?"

Funding for the makerspaces came from a variety of sources. Respondents chose one or more of the following ways that their makerspaces could be funded. Respondents were able to select more than one response, so the total percentage will be higher than 100 percent.

Table A.4. "Did the Funding to Start Your Makerspace Come From . . . ?"

	RESPONDENTS	
	n	%
The library budget	55	50
Grants	44	40
Donations	21	19
Additional funding from your parent organization	16	15
Other	16	15

"Do You Charge for Any of the Following Items in Your Makerspace?"

Thirty-four respondents (31 percent of all respondents) reported that their makerspaces charge (or will be charging) for items. Respondents were able to select more than one response, so the total percentage will be higher than 100 percent.

Table A.5. "Do You Charge for Any of the Following Items in Your Makerspace?"

	RESPONDENTS	
	n	%
Supplies used in making	22	65
Other	11	24
Fees for classes or workshops	7	21
Membership fee	3	9
Equipment use	2	6

"When People Ask You Why You Have a Makerspace, What Do You Tell Them?"

A selection of these comments is included in chapter 2.

"What Kinds of Tools or Equipment or Creation Options Does Your Makerspace Have?"

Table A.6. "What Kinds of Tools or Equipment or Creation Options Does Your Makerspace Have?"

	RESPONDENTS	
TECHNOLOGY/ACTIVITY	*n*	%
Computer workstations	73	67
3D printing	50	46
Photo editing	49	45
Video editing	47	43
Computer programming/software	43	39
Art and crafts	40	37
Scanning photos to digital	39	36
Creating a website or online portfolio	37	34
Digital music recording	36	33
3D modeling	34	31
Arduino/Raspberry Pi	33	30
Other	33	30
Animation	31	28
High quality scanner	31	28
Tinkering	28	26
Electronic music programming	26	24
Creating apps	24	22

TECHNOLOGY/ACTIVITY	RESPONDENTS	
	n	%
Game creation	24	22
Soldering iron	24	22
Electronics	23	21
Prototyping	21	19
Robotics	19	17
Fabric shop[a]	18	17
Circuit hacking	17	16
Digital scrapbooking	16	15
Electronic book production	15	14
Inventing	15	14
Soft circuits	15	14
VHS conversion equipment	14	13
Mobile development	13	12
Large format printer	9	8
Vinyl cutting	9	8
Laser cutting	8	7
Food/culinary arts	6	6
Screen printing	5	5
Woodworking[b]	4	4
Bicycle building/maintenance	3	3
Ceramics	3	3
Computerized numerical control machines	3	3
Jewelry making[c]	3	3
Plastics/composites	3	3
Dark room	2	2
Industrial sewing machine	2	2
Milling machine	2	2
Mold making	2	2
Automotive	1	1
Guitar repair	1	1
Potter's wheel and kiln	1	1
Silkscreening	1	1
Blacksmithing	0	0

(continued)

Table A.6. *(Continued)*

TECHNOLOGY/ACTIVITY	RESPONDENTS	
	n	%
Glass shop[d]	0	0
Letterpress	0	0
Metal shop[e]	0	0
Stained glass	0	0
Welding	0	0

[a] Sewing machines, leather sewing machines, computerized numerical control embroidery, etc.

[b] Table saw, panel saw, bandsaw, drill press, belt sanders, etc.

[c] Acetylene torch, buffing station, annealing pans, forming tools, metal smithing, etc.

[d] Glass blowing, kiln, jewelry making, etc.

[e] Metal lathe, cold saw, horizontal bandsaw, sheet metal shear, etc.

Respondents were able to select more than one response, so the total percentage will be higher than 100 percent.

"How Did You Decide What Technologies to Offer in Your Makerspace?"

Table A.7. "How Did You Decide What Technologies to Offer in Your Makerspace?"

	RESPONDENTS	
	n	%
Modeled on other makerspaces	56	51
Input from educators	46	42
Suggestions from patrons	33	30
Other	27	25
Patron surveys	17	16
Donations of equipment	15	14

Respondents were able to select more than one response, so the total percentage will be higher than 100 percent.

"What Items or Technologies Get the Most Use in Your Makerspace?"

A selection of these comments is included in chapter 4.

"What Kinds of Classes, Workshops, or Training Do You Provide in or for Your Makerspace?"

A selection of these comments is included in chapter 11.

"Are Trainings, Workshops, or Classes Taught By . . . ?"

Table A.8. "Are Trainings, Workshops, or Classes Taught by . . . ?"

	RESPONDENTS	
	n	%
Library staff	76	70
Volunteers	42	39
Paid instructors from beyond the library	20	18
Other	18	17

Respondents were able to select more than one response, so the total percentage will be higher than 100 percent.

"What Are Your Go-To Resources to Stay Aware of Developments That Could Impact Your Makerspace?"

A selection of these comments is included in chapter 12.

"What Do You Hope to Add to Your Makerspace in the Next Year?"

A selection of these comments is included in chapter 4.

Bibliography

"3D Printer Comparison." 2014. Maker Shed. http://www.makershed.com/Articles.asp?ID=301.

Abram, Stephen. 2013. "Makerspaces in Libraries, Education, and Beyond." *Internet@Schools* 20 (2): 18.

Anderson, Chris. 2012. *Makers: The New Industrial Revolution*. London: Random House Business Books.

———. 2013. "Maker Movement." *Wired* 21 (5): 106.

"Arapahoe Library Lets Patrons Borrow Recording Studio." 2013. *9News*. February 3. http://www.9news.com/news/local/article/314508/346/Arapahoe-Library-lets-patrons-borrow-recording-studio.

Bagley, Caitlin A. 2013. "Jeff Sturges on Libraries and Makerspaces." *ALA TechSource* (blog). February 15. http://www.alatechsource.org/blog/2013/02/jeff-sturges-on-libraries-and-makerspaces.html.

Barone, Meg. 2014. "High-Tech Quilting Project Knits Together Westport Community." *West-Port-News*. January 20. http://www.westport-news.com/news/article/High-tech-quilting-project-knits-together-5158843.php.

Belbin, Nicole, and Pat Newcombe. 2012. "Fab Labs at the Library." *Government Technology* 25 (10): 30–33.

Bhargava, Jennifer. 2012. "Hog Butchering Shows What Else a Library Might Be for These Days." *Kansas City Star* (blog). November 8. http://web.archive.org/web/20130123104619/http://joco913.com/news/hog-butchering-shows-what-a-library-might-be-for-these-day/.

Booth, Char. 2011. "Love Your Library Button Templates (and More): Project Curve, Part One Revisited." *Info-Mational* (blog). September 14. http://infomational.wordpress.com/2011/09/14/love-your-library-button-templates-and-more-project-curve-part-one-revisited/.

Britton, Lauren. 2012a. "A Fabulous Laboratory." *Public Libraries* 52 (4): 30–33.

———. 2012b. "The Making of Maker Spaces, Part 1: Space for Creation, Not Just Consumption." *The Digital Shift* (blog). October 1. http://www.thedigitalshift.com/2012/10/public-services/the-makings-of-maker-spaces-part-1-space-for-creation-not-just-consumption/.

Britton, Lauren, and Sue Considine. 2012. "The Making of Maker Spaces, Part 3: A Fabulous Home for Cocreation." *The Digital Shift* (blog). October 1. http://www.thedigitalshift

.com/2012/10/public-services/the-makings-of-maker-spaces-part-3-a-fabulous-home-for-cocreation/.

Cash, Martin. 2011. "Making It . . . with a Little Help." *Winnipeg Free Press.* October 8, B6.

Causey, Jennifer. 2013. *Brooklyn Makers: Food, Design, Craft, and Other Scenes from a Tactile Life.* New York: Princeton Architectural Press.

Cavalcanti, Gui. 2013a. "Is It a Hackerspace, Makerspace, TechShop, or FabLab?" *Make:.* http://makezine.com/2013/05/22/the-difference-between-hackerspaces-makerspaces-techshops-and-fablabs/.

———. 2013b. "Making Makerspaces: Creating a Business Model." *Make:* (blog). June 4. http://makezine.com/2013/06/04/making-makerspaces-creating-a-business-model/.

Chang, Stephanie. 2013. "Three Transformative Tools: From Old Tech to New (Part 2)." *Makezine* (blog). July 16. http://makezine.com/2013/07/16/three-transformative-tools-from-old-tech-to-new-part-2/.

ClaudineK. 2014. "Upcycled Chandelier." Instructables.com. http://www.instructables.com/id/Upcycled-Chandelier/.

Colegrove, Tod. 2013. "Editorial Board Thoughts: Libraries as Makerspace?" *Information Technology & Libraries* 32 (1): 2–5.

"Cool Stuff to Outfit Your Makerspace." 2013. *American Libraries* 44 (1/2): 48–49.

Dean, Alexandra. 2012. "The DIY Movement Meets the VCs." *Bloomberg Businessweek* 4267: 55–56.

Doctorow, Cory. 2009. *Makers.* New York: Tor.

Dougherty, Dale. 2012. "The Maker Movement." *Innovations: Technology, Governance, Globalization* 7 (3): 11–14.

———. 2013. "The Maker Mindset." In *Design, Make, Play: Growing the Next Generation of STEM Innovators,* edited by Margaret Honey and David Kanter, 7–11. New York: Routledge.

Encheff, Dana. 2013. "Creating a Science E-Book with Fifth Grade Students." *Techtrends: Linking Research & Practice to Improve Learning* 57 (6): 61–72.

Farkas, Meredith. 2013. "In Practice. Spare Me the Hype Cycle." *American Libraries* 44 (5): 23.

Fletcher, Owen. 2013. "Check These Out at the Library: Blacksmithing, Bowling, Butchering." *Wall Street Journal Online.* January 7. http://online.wsj.com/news/articles/SB10001424127887324677204578187901423347828.

FutureMakers. 2012. "What Is Your Readiness for a Makerspace?" http://kidsmakethingsbetter.com/wp-content/uploads/2013/11/What-is-your-level-of-makerspace-readiness.pdf.

Gallant, Riel. 2013. "3D Printing in Libraries around the World." *3ders* (blog). April 22. http://www.3ders.org/articles/20130422-3d-printing-in-libraries-around-the-world.html.

Gershenfeld, Neil A. 2005. *Fab: The Coming Revolution on Your Desktop—From Personal Computers to Personal Fabrication.* New York: Basic Books.

"Getting Started." 2013. YOUmedia Network. http://www.youmedia.org/toolkit/getting-started.

Gilpin, Lyndsey. 2014. "3D Printing: Ten Factors Still Holding It Back." TechRepublic. February 19. http://www.techrepublic.com/article/3d-printing-10-factors-still-holding-it-back/.

Ginsberg, Sharona. 2013. "Mentors for Makers: Effective and Budget-Friendly." *MakerBridge* (blog). December 16. http://makerbridge.si.umich.edu/blog/131216-800.

Good, Travis. 2013a. "Making Makerspace Libraries." ILEADUSA2013. YouTube. March 28. http://www.youtube.com/watch?v=WV_Eu5Kz1cA&feature=youtu.be.

———. 2013b. "Three Makerspace Models That Work." *American Libraries* 44 (1/2): 45–47.

Gustafson, Ellen. 2013. "Meeting Needs: Makerspaces and School Libraries." *School Library Monthly* 29 (8): 35–36.

Gutsche, Betha. 2013. "Makerspaces in Libraries: Patron's Delight, Staff's Dread?" *Alki* 29 (1): 28–30.

Hammond, Keith. 2013. "Extreme LED Throwies." *Makezine* (blog). http://makezine.com/projects/extreme-led-throwies/.

Hanshaw, Angela. 2013. "Attract Teens to Your Library with Minecraft." *Programming Librarian* (blog). July 25. http://www.programminglibrarian.org/blog/2013/july-2013/attract-teens-to-your-library-with-minecraft.html.

Harris, Stephen. 2013. "Why Manufacturers Should Embrace the Maker Movement." *Engineer* 2. Online edition.

Hilton, Lisa. 2013. "Guerrilla Maker Space: An Interview with Emerging Designers." *Makezine* (blog). December 10. http://makezine.com/magazine/guerrilla-maker-space-an-interview-with-emerging-designers/.

"A History of Making." 2013. *American Libraries* 44 (1/2): 46.

Honey, Margaret, and Eric Siegel. 2011. "The Maker Movement." *Education Week* 30 (19): 32–25.

Janes, Joseph. 2013. "Another Story. Common Ground." *American Libraries* 44 (11/12): 22.

Jenkins, Henry. 2009. *Confronting the Challenges of Participatory Culture: Media Education for the 21st Century*. Cambridge, MA: MIT Press.

Jenkins, Henry, Sam Ford, and Joshua Green. 2013. *Spreadable Media: Creating Value and Meaning in a Networked Culture*. New York: New York University Press.

Kemp, Adam. 2013. *The Makerspace Workbench: Tools, Technologies, and Techniques for Making* Sebastopol, CA: Maker Media.

Kenney, Brian. 2013. "Meet Your Makers." *Publishers Weekly* 260 (13): 20.

KevinB. 2013. "Weekend Project: Planter Boxes!" MilwaukeeMakerspace.org. June 14. http://milwaukeemakerspace.org/2013/06/weekend-project-planter-boxes/.

Koningsbrugge, Ruud van. 2014. "Plastic Bottle Birdhouse." Instructables.com. http://www.instructables.com/id/Plastic-bottle-birdhouse/.

Kooistra, Durk. 2009. "Portable Mini Vocal Booth." Humanworkshop. August 15. http://humanworkshop.com/index.php?modus=e_zine&sub=articles&item=115.

LaRue, James. 2013. "Wanna Write a Good One? Library as Publisher." *American Libraries* (blog). June 25. http://www.americanlibrariesmagazine.org/article/wanna-write-good-one-library-publisher.

"Laser Cutter." 2013. Robots and Dinosaurs Hackerspace (wiki). July 8. http://hackerspace.pbworks.com/w/page/41180361/Lasercutter.

Levy, Steven. 2010. *Hackers: Heroes of the Computer Revolution*. Sebastopol, CA: O'Reilly Media.

Lipson, Hod, and Melba Kurman. 2013. *Fabricated: The New World of 3D Printing*. Indianapolis, IN: Wiley.

"Logo and Barcode Marked Aluminum." 2014. MELDWorkshop.com. http://meldworkshop.com/projects/logo-and-barcode-marked-aluminum.

Lucylollipop. 2014. "Metal Casting." Instructables.com. http://www.instructables.com/id/Metal-Casting/.

"The Maker Movement and Its Implications." 2013. *Trends Magazine* 119: 11–16.

Makerspace.com. 2013a. "Makerspace Playbook." http://makerspace.com/wp-content/uploads/2013/02/MakerspacePlaybook-Feb2013.pdf.

———. 2013b. "What's a Makerspace?" http://makerspace.com/home-page.

Martinez, Sylvia Libow, and Gary Stager. 2013. *Invent to Learn: Making, Tinkering, and Engineering in the Classroom*. Torrance, CA: Constructing Modern Knowledge Press.

Melgar, Enrique Ramos, and Ciriaco Castro Diez. 2012. *Arduino and Kinect Projects: Design, Build, and Blow Their Minds*. New York: Apress.

Michaelson, Elizabeth. 2013. "Toronto's Kitchen Library Brings Appliances to All." *Library Journal* (blog). November 5. http://lj.libraryjournal.com/2013/11/library-services/torontos-kitchen-library-brings-appliances-to-all/.

Nagata, Kazuaki. 2013. "Hands on with the 'Maker Movement.'" *Japan Times*. June 26. http://www.japantimes.co.jp/life/2013/06/26/lifestyle/hands-on-with-the-maker-movement/#.UxSqUPldVuI.

Old Bridge Public Library. 2014. "Old Bridge Public Library Awarded Contract to Build Idea Farm Makerspace." *Old Bridge Public Library* (blog). February 11. http://eastbrunswick

.patch.com/groups/old-bridge-public-library/p/old-bridge-public-library-awarded-contract-to-build-idea-farm-makerspace.

O'Neill, Terence, and Josh Williams. 2014a. *3D Printing*. Ann Arbor, MI: Cherry Lake.

———. 2014b. *Arduino*. Ann Arbor, MI: Cherry Lake.

Owens, Tammi. 2013. "Notes from LITA Forum 2013, Session 1." *Hundreds of Things* (blog). December 1. http://www.hundredsofthings.net/notes-from-lita-forum-2013-session-1/.

Parks, Bob. 2006. *Makers: All Kinds of People Making Amazing Things in Garages, Basements, and Backyards*. Sebastopol, CA: O'Reilly Media.

Programming Librarian. 2014. "National Culinary Arts Month." http://www.programminglibrarian.org/library/events-and-celebrations/national-culinary-arts-month.html.

Quinn, Brendan. 2013. "Collaboration, Teaching, and Technology in Northwestern University Library's Digital Collections Training Lab." In *The New Academic Librarian: Essays on Changing Roles and Responsibilities*, edited by Rebecca Peacock and Jill Wurm, 161–69. Jefferson, NC: McFarland & Company.

Rassette, Eden. 2014. "Easy Does It: A Pop-Up Teen Makerspace." *Library as Incubator Project* (blog). February 3. http://www.libraryasincubatorproject.org/?p=13181.

Resnick, Michael, and Eric Rosenbaum. 2013. "Designing for Tinkerability." In *Design, Make, Play: Growing the Next Generation of STEM Innovators*, edited by Margaret Honey and David Kanter, 163–81. New York: Routledge.

Richardson, Greg. 2013. "$6 Upcycled Dog Bed." *7hills Makerspace* (blog). October 12. http://7hillsmake.org/2013/10/12/6-upcycled-dog-bed/.

Roscorla, Tanya. 2013. "Why the 'Maker Movement' Is Popular in Schools." *Center for Digital Education* (blog). August 14. http://www.centerdigitaled.com/news/Maker-Movement-Popular-Schools.html.

Roslund, Samantha, and Emily Puckett Rodgers. 2014. *Makerspaces*. Ann Arbor, MI: Cherry Lake.

Sanchez, Joseph. 2013. "From Content Warehouse to Content Provider: Libraries at the Crossroads." http://www.thebookmyfriend.com/uploads/6/1/1/3/6113160/from_content_warehouse_to_content_producer_libraries_at_the_crossroads.pdf.

Sansing, Chad. 2013. "Life with Raspberry Pi: Sparking a School Coding Revolution." *The Digital Shift* (blog). August 19. http://www.thedigitalshift.com/2013/08/k-12/life-with-raspberry-pi-this-slim-25-computer-is-hot-and-showing-no-signs-of-cooling-off-it-may-just-spark-a-coding-revolution-in-schools/.

Schwartz, Meredith. 2012. "Let Them Lend Cake Pans." *Library Journal* (blog). June 14. http://lj.libraryjournal.com/2012/06/library-services/let-them-lend-cake-pans/.

Shapiro, Phil. 2013. "A Librarian's Guide to Boosting the Maker Movement." Makezine.com. August 28. http://makezine.com/2013/08/28/a-librarians-guide-to-boosting-the-maker-movement/.

Smith, Grace. 2013. "Ten Excellent Platforms for Building Mobile Apps." *Mashable.com* (blog). December 3. http://mashable.com/2013/12/03/build-mobile-apps/.

Sousa, David A., and Thomas Pilecki. 2013. *From STEM to STEAM: Using Brain-Compatible Strategies to Integrate the Arts*. Thousand Oaks, CA: Corwin Press.

Sparkleponytx. 2014. "5 Things to Do with an Old Shirt." Instructables.com. http://www.instructables.com/id/5-Things-to-Do-with-An-Old-Shirt/.

Stager, G. S. 2013. "Papert's Prison Fab Lab: Implications for the Maker Movement and Education Design." In *Proceedings of the 12th International Conference on Interaction Design and Children*, 487–90. New York: ACM.

Stark, Chelsea. 2012. "How iBooks Author Stacks Up to the Competition." *Mashable.com* (blog). January 23. http://mashable.com/2012/01/23/ibooks-author-self-publishing-comparison/.

Tait, Barbara, and K-Fai Steele. 2014. "Make Jawn at the Free Library of Philadelphia: Emerging Best Practices for Maker Programming in Libraries." *Library as Incubator Project* (blog). January 27. http://www.libraryasincubatorproject.org/?p=13186.

Thomas, AnnMarie. 2013. "Squishy Circuits." In *Design, Make, Play: Growing the Next Generation of STEM Innovators*, edited by Margaret Honey and David Kanter, 119–37. New York: Routledge.

Thompson, Clive, and Carin Goldberg. 2013. "The Fixer Movement Repair All Your Broken Stuff, Save the World." *Wired* 21 (7): 74.

Torrone, Phillip. 2011. "Is It Time to Rebuild & Retool Public Libraries and Make 'TechShops'?" *Make:*. March 3. http://makezine.com/2011/03/10/is-it-time-to-rebuild-retool-public-libraries-and-make-techshops/.

Valenza, Joyce. 2008. "Library as Domestic Metaphor." *Neverending Search* (blog). August 25. http://blogs.slj.com/neverendingsearch/2008/08/25/library-as-domestic-metaphor/.

Watters, Audrey. 2013. "The Case for a Campus Makerspace." *Hack Education* (blog). February 6. http://hackeducation.com/2013/02/06/the-case-for-a-campus-makerspace/.

Westport Library. 2014. "Maker-in-Residence." http://westportlibrary.org/maker-residence.

Wilkinson, Karen, and Mike Petrich. 2014. *The Art of Tinkering*. San Francisco, CA: Weldon Owen.

Woodbury, David, and Ian Charnas. 2013. "Fostering a Place for Invention and Creation: Two Approaches to Makerspaces on Campus." EDUCAUSE (Webinar). October 28. http://www.educause.edu/library/resources/fostering-place-invention-and-creation-two-approaches-makerspaces-campus.

Index

About the Author

John J. Burke holds the rank of principal librarian and is the director of the Gardner-Harvey Library on the Middletown regional campus of Miami University (Ohio). He has a master in library science from the University of Tennessee and a bachelor of arts in history from Michigan State University. John is a past president of the Academic Library Association of Ohio and past chair of the Southwest Ohio Council on Higher Education Library Council. His past work includes service as both systems/public services librarian and program director for a web-based associate degree in library technology at the University of Cincinnati–Raymond Walters College and as a reference and electronic resources librarian at Fairmont State College (WV). He is the author of four editions of the *Neal-Schuman Library Technology Companion: A Basic Guide for Library Staff* (2001, 2006, 2009, 2013), as well as *Embedding Librarianship in Learning Management Systems* (with Beth Tumbleson; 2013), *IntroNet: A Beginner's Guide to Searching the Internet* (1999), and *Learning the Internet: A Workbook for Beginners* (1996). He has presented on a variety of technology topics at conferences held by the Association of College and Research Libraries and the Academic Library Association, the LITA National Forum, and various regional and state conferences. John may be reached at techcompanion@gmail.com.